ON REFLECTION

ON REFLECTION

An Essay on Technology, Education,
and the Status of Thought in the Twenty-First Century

ELLEN ROSE

Canadian Scholars' Press Inc.
Toronto

On Reflection: An Essay on Technology, Education,
and the Status of Thought in the Twenty-First Century

Ellen Rose

First published in 2013 by
Canadian Scholars' Press Inc.
425 Adelaide Street West, Suite 200
Toronto, Ontario
M5V 3C1

www.cspi.org

Canadian Scholars' Press Inc. gratefully acknowledges financial support
for our publishing activities from the Government of Canada through
the Canada Book Fund (CBF).

Library and Archives Canada Cataloguing in Publication

Rose, Ellen, 1959–
On reflection : an essay on technology, education, and
the status of thought in the 21st century / Ellen Rose.

Includes bibliographical references and index.
Also issued in electronic format.
ISBN 978-1-55130-518-9

1. Critical thinking. I. Title.

B809.2.R68 2013   160   C2012-906614-1

Text design by Susan MacGregor/Digital Zone
Cover design by Gordon Robertson
Cover image: tomograf © iStockphoto

14 15 16 17   5 4 3 2

Printed and bound in Canada by Webcom

Canada

CONTENTS

INTRODUCTION

SEVERAL YEARS AGO, I CO-TAUGHT A PARTICULARLY MEMORABLE doctoral seminar. The six PhD students were also teachers: some taught elementary grades, some taught middle or high school; all had recently taken a leave of absence from their teaching to pursue doctoral studies. One afternoon, one of the teacher-students gave an informal presentation on a pedagogical process, what it was now eludes me, in which the penultimate step was "reflection." However, I do recall distinctly that, as the presenter described this step and its importance, one of the other teachers laughed. "Yeah, right," she said, "like we have time for reflection!" The others chuckled appreciatively, and the presentation continued.

I am sure that no one else sitting around the seminar table that afternoon would recall this episode now, but for me it was a decisive moment. I had already begun thinking about the concept of "reflection," a word that liberally dots the pages of much contemporary educational discourse, including the books and articles about educational technology with which I spend much of my time. Despite its frequent appearance, however, the word tends to be used vaguely and imprecisely, rarely in a way that makes clear what is meant or even why exactly reflection matters. My ponderings on the subject up to that point seemed to partake of this amorphous quality: they were confined to vague, undirected questions about what reflection entailed. I was not even sure that it was a topic I should be wasting my time think-ing about, given that everyone else seemed to take for granted that we all share a common understanding of what reflection is and why it is important.

That snippet of conversation, however, served to crystallize my contemplations. Here was a group of individuals who, as both teachers and graduate students, had freely and somewhat cavalierly acknowledged that reflection could play no part in their lives. This seemed to me to be a matter for some concern. What does it mean when those who presumably play a sig-nificant role in shaping children's habits of mind admit that the nature of their work mitigates against the ability to stop and think? When university students seeking the highest level of education possible, Doctor of Philosophy, casually dismiss reflective thought in this way? Sitting at that seminar table, it was brought home to me that my questions about reflection were really questions about what education is and should be, and were therefore worth asking.

But, of course, the issue goes beyond teachers. In this day and age, how many people, I asked myself, really do reflect in the course of a day, a week, a year, a lifetime? I recalled a businessman with whom, some time ago, I commiserated because of his two-hour commute to and from work every day. "Actually," he had replied, "I find it gives me an opportunity to think about things." Is this, I wondered, what reflection has become? Is gripping the steering wheel and navigating traffic or travelling through space at 100 kilometres an hour the closest we can now come to stopping and thinking?

I carried this question into my classroom, where I asked my students, young adults in their late teens and early twen-ties, how much time they spent engaged in reflective thought.

None, they told me, laughing. It was the same laughter I had heard from the teachers: both rueful and dismissive. It was the laughter of people who were, it seemed to me, literally trying to "laugh off" something over which they believed themselves to have no control. I spoke to many other people—teachers, university professors, parents, business people, artists—and found the same answer over and over again. One person sheepishly admitted going to the funeral of a respected colleague and reveling in the opportunity to sit in the peace and quiet of the church: "I thought, this is really too bad—that, in order to reflect, I have to go to a funeral!"

The essay that follows is a reflection on reflection. It traces my journey toward an understanding of reflection and its proper role in our educational institutions and processes, and in our lives. Like all journeys, it is idiosyncratic. My specific interests in media and technology have shaped its direction, although I am convinced that no thoughtful treatment of reflection today can avoid a consideration of the ways in which our modes of communication impinge upon the ways that we think and the things that we think about. In fact, it is a fundamental premise of this book that the technologies that support human interaction and knowledge acquisition are implicated in some profound changes in habits of mind.

The journey begins with an attempt to come to terms with what reflection is. This is not the straightforward task it might seem, for the word has in recent years undergone a significant and yet largely unremarked transformation. This transformation owes much to the work of John Dewey and Donald Schön, two philosophers who sought at different times to redefine reflection as action: scientific process and on-the-spot decision making, respectively. In Chapter 1, I establish that my intention is to reclaim an understanding of reflection as a form of deep thought that takes place in conditions of solitude and slowness.

In Chapter 2, I take up the question of why reflection matters. Elaborating on the definition provided in Chapter 1, I characterize reflection as a generative mode of thought and therefore the basis of creativity, insight, and new ways of thinking about the world and ourselves. Reflection matters, I further argue, because contemplations that take place in retreat from the social world may very well lead to a revisioning of that world—indeed, they may inspire action that is informed by both mindful attention to traditional praxis and engagement with the present. On this basis, I propose that the relationship between reflection and action is best characterized not as Schön's reflection-in-action nor even as reflection-on-action, but as reflection-then-action, in which periods of reflection give rise to small actions that, in their cumulative effect, restore personal and social balance and integrity.

Chapter 3 takes a historical turn, tracing the rise of reflection and relating it to two technologies that enabled private reading and introspection: the alphabet and the printing press. A key premise of this book is that the arrival of new communications technologies, from the alphabet to the Internet, leads to gradual but definite changes in social relations and habits of mind. Building upon this premise, this chapter outlines how the emergence of the alphabet and the printing press gave rise to a literate public newly empowered to both create and gain knowledge independently, apart from ritualized social practices. As books became the chief means by which knowledge was circulated, new modes of thinking became possible: scientific thought flourished, speculative thought gave rise to the novel and other fictional forms, and, where the conditions of slowness and solitude prevailed, people became increasingly able and inclined to reflect.

Having established that literacy and typography played a key role in giving rise to the reflective intellect, I ask in Chapter 4 if this causal relationship persists at the level of the individual. In other words, is there an interrelation among reading, writing, and reflection? And if there is a connection, as many experts insist, then does the growing phenomenon of aliteracy, manifested when capable readers choose not to read, presage a decline in reflective thought?

In Chapter 5, I confront some of the gloomy assessments of the state of thought in the twenty-first century. Signs of the decline of reflection surround us, particularly in the realm of human communications, where we regularly encounter political discourse, news, and business transactions that are becoming increasingly banal, frivolous, and rushed. In the classroom, the pressing demands of curriculum coverage increasingly detract from time in which both teachers and learners can simply stop and think. But if reflection is falling by the wayside, is it because we no longer choose to engage in deep, slow thought? Or is it because, in a world in which the pace of human activity is increasingly dictated by our digital devices, our wired brains are simply no longer capable of silent reverie?

There is no doubt that, today, one of the chief obstacles to reflection is information technology, and as such it warrants a chapter of its own. Chapter 6 therefore explores how new technologies work against the reflective intellect that arose with the alphabet and flourished after the invention of the printing press. In particular, as social life is increasingly transferred online, more and more of us live in a state of what has been called "hyper attention" or "continuous partial attention," which severely mitigates against the tendency to stop and think, and which therefore has profound implications for teaching and learning.

In Chapter 7, I discuss the difference between schooling and education and confront the challenges of fostering reflection within school settings, which are often inimical to the development and flourishing of the reflective mind.

Acknowledgements

I wish to extend my sincere gratitude to the many people who took the time to talk to me about reflection during the many years that I thought about and worked on this project. Your encouragement and enthusiasm for the topic were inspiring, and my reflections upon reflection were vastly enriched by your insights and diverse perspectives. Special thanks to those who generously consented to participate in interviews and allowed me to share their insights and perspectives on reflection in this book. I also wish to give special acknowledgement to Heather Menzies and Stephanie Bennett, who read early drafts and offered sage advice and encouragement; to the anonymous readers of my manuscript, for their helpful comments and suggestions; and above all and always, to my husband, Tony Tremblay, for his wise and loving support.

Chapter 1

RECLAIMING REFLECTION

We must give thought to what reflection means.[1]

—Martin Heidegger

WHAT IS REFLECTION? ALTHOUGH THE WORD APPEARS OFTEN in the discourse of education, it remains slippery, continually wriggling free of a clear and consistent meaning. One reason for its elusiveness as a signifier may have to do with the profound transformations in meaning reflection has undergone over the past four or five centuries.

Dictionaries and etymologies tell us that the word comes from the Latin *reflectere*: *re* meaning "back" and *flectere* meaning "to bend." Until the seventeenth century, reflection was largely used to describe the image that was cast back when light hit a reflective surface such as glass or water. In the early 1600s, a new meaning emerged, at least in part as a result of the transformations in society and thought inaugurated by the printing press that I describe in Chapter 3. Etymologies suggest that in 1605 the verb "reflect" was first used to refer to the act of turning one's thought to something, rather than to an optical phenomenon, and by the 1650s, "reflection" was being used to describe a remark made after turning one's thought to a subject. In *An Essay Concerning Human Understanding*, published in 1690, philosopher John Locke used reflection to denote the natural human propensity to turn one's thoughts upon one's own thought processes, which he offered as a primary source of ideas. Soon thereafter, reflection became synonymous with a deep or serious consideration of ideas, the kind of independent, careful thought that had become possible—indeed, highly desirable—in the new print culture. Eventually, the original meaning of reflection, a bending or turning back, became obsolete.

Etymologies and dictionary definitions offer a useful starting point, but as I read them, I cannot help but feel that they omit something important. Certainly, reflection denotes careful consideration and contemplation, but it *connotes* a great deal more. What does reflection mean to me? When I close my eyes and try to picture reflection, I immediately envision someone sitting in a book-lined room, reading or pondering silently. It is clear that, for me, reflection entails something more than careful thought: it connotes quietude, solitude, and a leisurely involvement with ideas.

When I talk with other people, I find that they all define reflection in unique ways: the book-lined room appears to be mine alone. But the themes of quietude and solitude crop up repeatedly. Reflection, I am told, is something that happens "in the privacy of your own mind and your own space." I find these themes repeated in my reading. When, in the 1850s, author Henry David Thoreau wanted to "live deliberately, to front only the essential facts of life,"[2] he retired to an old farmhouse on Walden Pond, whose chief attraction was "its complete retirement, being . . . half a mile from the nearest neighbor."[3] Writing over 150 years later, Robert Pogue Harrison, a Stanford University professor of Italian literature, offers the garden as the ideal reflective space because it "makes room for what the bustling world tends to crowd out or stifle. It makes room for thought, vision, recollection, reverie, and the sort of deep time that is the natural element of such psychic phenomena."[4] And philosopher Hannah Arendt evokes a figurative space when she describes the contemplative way of life as consisting of "sheer quietness . . . in the 'desert.'"[5] My book-lined room, Thoreau's farmhouse in the woods, Harrison's cultivated garden, and Arendt's figurative desert are all very different spaces, but they share two important qualities: they are silent and they offer the individual the opportunity to withdraw momentarily from the world's ceaseless hubbub.

Time is also a recurrent theme in everything I read and hear on the subject. Reflective time is necessarily slow. Slow, of course, not in the sense that our fast-paced world tends to define it, as synonymous with laziness or stupidity, but a slowness that is associated with the increasingly rare qualities of care and attentiveness. Rare because, in general, the modern world demands hasty thought. Survival, in so many jobs today, seems to depend upon an ability to "think on one's feet," "hit the ground running," and "make rapid-fire decisions." Reflective thought is the exception to this rule: reflection unfolds slowly, in its own good time, during periods of stillness seized from the bustle and busyness of everyday life. And because it takes place over time—or even, I might say, outside the demands and constraints of time—reflection entails a depth of understanding quite contrary to the superficial grasp of a situation or idea to which we are limited by snap decisions and split-second thinking.

This, then, is the essence of reflection, the reflection that I want to reclaim in this chapter, and in this book as a whole: a form of deep, sustained thought for which the necessary preconditions are solitude and slowness.

* * *

Why must I reclaim this meaning of reflection? Because words tend to be as elusive and changeable as chameleons. I am not referring to changes in meaning that take place over centuries. These changes, like those that have occurred in the meaning of reflection since the seventeenth century, are inevitable and natural in a living language. But words can also undergo extreme and yet largely unnoticed changes in far shorter order. This is what is now happening to reflection, which, as it crops up more and more in educational discourse, seems to become increasingly difficult to pin down.

In fact, in the field of education there are many examples of such chameleon words undergoing subtle but significant transformations that do not show up in dictionaries or etymologies. For example, consider the words "mind" and "intelligence." Hank Bromley, an astute commentator on the politics of technology, observes that these words have been taken down a notch in recent years with the rise of research and discourse on artificial intelligence: "Since actually replicating human intelligence on a machine is such a formidable task, what happens instead is the redefinition of 'mind' down to a lower level that *can* be imitated by machines."[6] Similar transformations have taken place with other words whose meanings play a vital role in constructing our understanding of what the enterprise of education is and should be—words like "literacy," "knowledge," and even "wisdom." Marc Prensky, a popular speaker on technology and learning, recently (and, to my mind, shockingly) redefined wisdom as a "complex kind of problem solving"[7] that can be enhanced by technology. We can expect these and other words to continue to undergo severe metamorphoses in meaning as human learning is increasingly characterized as information processing and the digital devices around us as "smart."

Why is the meaning of reflection changing? Quite simply, because in our digital-cellular-online-robotic-information-saturated-hyper society, solitude and slowness are increasingly difficult to come by. We all share in this predicament. As Heather Menzies cogently argues in *No Time: Stress and the Crisis of Modern Life*, excessive busyness has become the zeitgeist of the modern world. One way of responding to the growing impossibility of reflection is to redefine it.

But before discussing how reflection is being redefined, largely without notice, I want to consider two other common responses to the growing impossibility of reflection. One is to do what those teachers at the seminar table did: to "laugh off" demands that we stop and think. Laughing off can quickly give way to laughing *at* those rare individuals who are devoted to a contemplative way of life. In this way, characters such as the socially alienated and dysfunctional philosopher, the absent-minded professor, and the bookish child become figures of fun. They are comically transmuted into bumbling fools and clichéd embodiments of a tacit consensus that reflection no longer has any place in our chaotic, hectic "real" lives, in which solitude and slowness have given way to ceaseless commerce, bustling bureaucracies, and hectic workdays amidst the ubiquitous drone of technological devices.

Such laughter is a form of self-saving repudiation, but it contains a chilly note of hostility and condemnation that author Alberto Manguel captures beautifully in his memories of being a bookish child:

> I remember being laughed at, during one recess in grade six or seven, for staying indoors and reading, and how the taunting ended with me sprawled face down on the floor, my glasses kicked into one corner, my book into another. . . . My grandmother, seeing me read on Sunday

afternoons, would sigh, "You're day-dreaming," because
my inactivity seemed to her a wasteful idleness and sin
against the joy of living. Slothful, feeble, pretentious,
pedantic, elitist—these are some of the epithets that eventually became associated with the absent-minded scholar,
the poor-sighted reader, the bookworm, the nerd. Buried in
books, isolated from the world of facts and flesh, superior
to those unfamiliar with words preserved between dusty
covers, the bespectacled reader who pretended to know
what God in His wisdom had hidden was seen as a fool,
and glasses became emblematic of intellectual arrogance.[8]

What is going on here? As philosopher Martin Heidegger
puts it, reflective thought is being dismissed as something that
is "out-of-order," a disruption of "the familiar order of the
everyday."[9] I find this troubling because it suggests the depth
of the chasm that has arisen between "real life" and reflection.
Increasingly, the latter is regarded as a mode of thought available only to philosophers, academics, and those other fortunate
few (lighthouse keepers, perhaps!) who are able to achieve the
requisite solitude and slowness—in short, those who have the
luxury of disregarding, for extended periods, the practicalities
and manufactured urgencies of everyday life. For the rest of us,
reflection is out-of-order. The judicial connotation of Heidegger's
phrase is apt. Like someone making an uncalled-for interruption
in a courtroom, the reflective individual is held "in contempt"
by contemporary society for failing to contribute anything of
utilitarian value to the work that must be done—and this is a
grave offence in a society like ours, which gives so much precedence to productivity, efficiency, and tangible results.

This leads to a second common response to the growing
impossibility of reflection: an attempt to blunt the edge of its

apparent elitism by fragmenting it into multiple levels and approaches. Many of the people with whom I have spoken on the subject, educators in particular, are inclined to speculate hopefully, or even to insist, that reflection is not a unitary phenomenon but essentially a skill that each person performs in his or her own way, in accordance with his or her particular situation, preferences, learning style, and capabilities. Thus, there is a willingness to accept such diverse phenomena as group brainstorming sessions, online discussions, and thinking on one's feet in the workplace as instances of reflection. This openness to finding traces of reflection in a range of activities and modes of thought emerges from a generous impulse. Whereas laughter excludes, the intention here is to include everything and everyone. The effect, however, is much the same: the diminishment of personal and social commitment to reflection as a form of thought that takes place within solitude and slowness.

This brings us back to redefinition. Given the hectic daily reality with which so many of us live, it is perhaps natural that we seek to bring reflection back into the realm of the possible by subtly, and sometimes not so subtly, altering its meaning. In this way, reflection is reconceived as something that we *can* do, even as we struggle with the contingencies of our busy lives. I have already commented upon Marc Prensky's redefinition of wisdom. He wreaks similar changes to the meaning of reflection in the following passage from a paper on "digital natives," those who grow up in front of the screen. In answer to the titular question, "Do they really *think* differently?" Prensky observes,

> One key area that appears to have been affected is reflection. . . . In our twitch-speed world, there is less and less time and opportunity for reflection, and this development concerns many people. One of the most interesting

> challenges and opportunities in teaching Digital Natives
> is to figure out and invent ways to include reflection and
> critical thinking in the learning (either built into the
> instruction or through a process of instructor-led debrief-
> ing) but still do it in the Digital Native language.[10]

Is Prensky suggesting that we help so-called digital natives
achieve reflection in the sense that I am seeking to reclaim,
the reflection of solitude and slowness? No, far from it. Rather,
he is arguing that we need to redefine reflection in ways that
accord with young people's capabilities and interests and the
demands of "our twitch-speed world." Further, he mistakenly
equates reflection with critical thinking, a purposeful, analytic
form of thought that entails taking things apart—deconstructing discourses, arguments, and systems of thought in order
to escape, as one textbook on critical thinking nicely puts it,
"the snares of dogma"[11]—whereas, as I will suggest in the next
chapter, the essence of reflection is synthesis: the creation of
new ideas, perspectives, and possibilities.

* * *

Why, we may wonder, does Prensky's suggestion that we radically
redefine reflection go unremarked? One reason is that far more
influential thinkers began wreaking even more profound changes
upon the meaning of reflection long before he came along.

In fact, the first notable attempt to redefine reflection was
launched by John Dewey in 1910 with the publication of *How
We Think*. Subtitled, in its 1933 reissue, *A Restatement of the
Relation of Reflective Thinking to the Educative Process*, the purpose of Dewey's influential book is to emphasize that promoting reflective thinking should be a primary aim of education.
But Dewey takes great liberties with the meaning of reflection.

Dismissing the centuries-old conventional understanding of the word as denoting, and connoting, a deliberative, contemplative state of mind, Dewey directly associates reflection with "that attitude of mind, that habit of thought, which we call scientific."[12]

Dewey belonged to a school of thought called pragmatism, a philosophical movement that shunned pure philosophy—that is, reflection for reflection's sake. Pragmatism was founded on the conviction that only ideas with practical implications have merit and are worth exploring. In this view, random, uncontrolled reverie about ideas with no practical bearing on the world "may be harmful to the mind," as Dewey argues, "because it distracts attention from the real world, and because it may be a waste of time."[13] Given his belief in the value of practical, useful action, it is no wonder that Dewey dismisses the conventional notion of reflection, entailing solitary, silent reverie, as nothing more than an irrelevant ramble in a field of "*mere* ideas, idle speculations, fantasies, dreams."[14] Nor is it any surprise that he then proceeds to co-opt the term for his own purposes.

In Dewey's lexicon, which would soon be adopted by many educators, reflection is redefined as a goal-driven, orderly problem-solving process instigated by a state of perplexity or mental doubt. He writes (and the emphatic italics are his), "*The function of reflective thought is, therefore, to transform a situation in which there is experienced obscurity, doubt, conflict, disturbance of some sort, into a situation that is clear, coherent, settled, harmonious.*"[15] This harmonious state can be reached through a "systematized method" consisting of five phases. In the first phase, confronted with a difficulty, "the mind leaps forward"[16] and comes up with a number of possible suggestions. In the second phase, the difficulty is reconceptualized as a problem to be solved. In the third phase, the reflective mind comes up with possible solutions and working hypotheses. The fourth phase involves reasoning and elaborating on the hypotheses, by means of which some may be discovered to be unsound and eliminated. Finally, in the fifth phase, the hypothesis that is most likely to solve the problem is tested by action.[17]

Action is a key element of Dewey's reflection. He seeks to disassociate himself from the conventional view of reflection as "not an activity but a passivity."[18] In place of a seemingly passive (for the mind, of course, is active) and random engagement with ideas, he offers a reflection—or, to use the gerund form that he preferred, a "reflective thinking"—that goes hand-in-hand with structured, scientific action. In Dewey's terms, reflection within conditions of slowness and solitude gives way to purposeful activity that can be applied to actual situations, and the reflective individual who seeks only to understand the world morphs into a problem-solver, actively engaged in changing the world. "Intelligent action"[19]—and, in particular, the action of following the five steps in the orderly problem-solving process—is synonymous with reflection, as Dewey redefines it.

According to philosopher Mortimer Adler, Dewey's fundamental error is "an exaggeration of the scientific method, which stresses investigation or research as if it were the only occasion for thought."[20] Nevertheless, Dewey's implicit condemnation of the educational status quo, in which "ideas have become so remote from objects and acts of experience that they are empty,"[21] and his insistence that significant educational improvements could be realized if children were taught to think scientifically, were very well received by North American society in the early twentieth century. This was a society, after all, that was increasingly prone to regard science as the primary source of knowledge, truth, and authority; that celebrated technology as its sole hope for progress; and, at the same time, blamed inadequate schooling for all its woes. In fact, as Adler further observes, *How We Think* was so well received that it went on to become "the bible for thousands of teachers."[22]

It was no surprise, then, that in the decades that followed, Dewey's instrumental, positivist definition of reflection gained popularity and superseded, at least among educators, the previous understanding of reflection as entailing quiet, solitary contemplation. Most subsequent educational publications on the subject—and there are many—cite Dewey or otherwise invoke his understanding of reflection as action, often undertaken collaboratively rather than by solitary individuals. For example, according to the authors of *An Introduction to Reflective Thinking*, published in 1923, reflection is always direct and purposeful, entirely the opposite of "rambling" thought with no particular outcome. Acknowledging their debt to Dewey, they write, "When thought . . . is bent on solving a problem, on finding out the meaning of a perplexing situation, or reaching a conclusion which is trustworthy, it is to be distinguished from other types of mental activity and should be called reflection."[23] Similarly, in *Reflective Thinking*, published in 1961, authors Henry Gordon Hullfish and Philip Smith echo Dewey, offering reflective activity as a process (now four phases instead of five) and asserting that "Reflection differs from the looser kinds of thinking primarily by virtue of being directed or controlled by a purpose—the solution of a problem."[24] And the editors of a 1985 collection, *Reflection: Turning Experience into Learning*, describe "reflective activity" as "not idle meanderings or day-dreaming,"[25] but a goal-directed, purposeful process, now reduced to three stages: preparation, engagement in an activity, and active processing of the experience.[26] Reflection, they add, "does not have to be a solitary activity."[27]

* * *

Dewey's redefinition of reflection prevailed until 1983, when Donald Schön launched the second major sally against conventional understandings of the word with the publication of his equally influential book, *The Reflective Practitioner*. Schön begins his book with a critique of what he calls "technical rationality," the view that "professional activity consists in instrumental problem solving made rigorous by the application of scientific theory and technique."[28] While Dewey is not named specifically, it is clear that Schön is rejecting the conflation of reflection with scientific process. In his view, a great deal of human experience defies the tidy problem-solving model to which Dewey reduces reflection. Schön argues that seeing the world in these terms, as presenting neatly packaged problems to be solved through an orderly process, is misleading because sometimes there is no clear problem, only confusion and complexity, and it is precisely in such fuzzy situations that the ability of the professional practitioner to engage in reflective thinking becomes vital.

But Schön also rejects the more conventional sense of reflection as entailing solitude and slowness. These might be preconditions for what Schön calls "reflection-on-action"—that is, stopping to engage in a retrospective contemplation of one's actions after the fact. But in Schön's view, thinking and doing are not mutually exclusive domains; rather, they can coexist as a form of intelligent action that Schön labels "reflection-*in*-action." Reflection-in-action refers to a professional's ability to think about his or her spontaneous response to a unique or unstable situation while actually engaged in making that response. In coping with such situations, Schön observes, professionals (such as teachers, doctors, and business people) tend to respond intuitively, and the professional knowledge guiding their actions tends to remain tacit. (This, of course, is the basic tenet upon which Malcolm Gladwell's 2005 book, *Blink: The Power of Thinking Without Thinking*, is based. The instant popularity of a book whose core message is that reflection is unnecessary—indeed, that snap judgments are often better than considered ones—says much about contemporary attitudes to slow, careful thought.) Schön's reflection-in-action involves taking professional knowledge out of the tacit realm: it happens when one notices at the time of action what one is doing and thinks about one's reasons for doing it. Because reflection-in-action entails social action in crisis situations and might take place during a split-second lull in the midst of the action, it is totally at odds with the notion of reflection as entailing solitude and slowness.

Despite their differences, then, Schön's and Dewey's redefinitions of reflection both equate reflection with doing and suggest that it is fundamentally inseparable from scientific or professional action.

Another important point of similarity between the two is that both have had the effect, intended or not, of knocking reflection from its pedestal of elitism. They accomplished this by redefining it as a mode of thought, involving either structured problem solving or split-second decision making, that is an intrinsic part of everyday life in which anyone can, and likely does, engage—even people whose daily round seems to consist entirely of a hectic whirl in which there is little opportunity to actually stop and think. As one commentator puts it, "the practice of reflection has experienced a rebirth of sorts by shedding the lofty wings of philosophical speculation and plunging into the murky well-waters of everyday life."[29]

This apparent democratization of reflection may seem, at first glance, to be a positive outcome. But the problem is that while we all now have an equal opportunity to engage in reflective thinking, as it is redefined by Dewey or by Schön, most of us are even more alienated from reflection in its conventional sense, the sense that I want to reclaim in this essay: reflection as thought that takes place within conditions of solitude and slowness. This is because, although Dewey and Schön both reject the Cartesian split between body and mind, between action and thought, their theorizing has the ultimate effect of enlarging the perceived gulf between real life and reflection. If it is possible to reflect on the go, in the midst of action, then making time to stop and think can only be increasingly regarded as a frivolous indulgence rather than something that it is necessary to do in order to live a sane and meaningful life.

I am all for abolishing the false opposition between contemplation and utility, between reflection and "real" life. But not by demanding that reflection become something that it is not: practical, action-oriented, solution-driven. Rather, we should begin to scrutinize our attitudes toward the reflection of solitude and slowness. For surely something is gravely amiss in the world when, in the words of Hannah Arendt, "the quest for meaning— as opposed to the thirst for knowledge" is "felt to be unnatural, as though men, whenever they reflect without purpose, . . . [are] engaged in an activity *contrary to the human condition.*"[30]

* * *

As Dewey's and Schön's ideas of reflective action seized hold of the public imagination, the meaning of the word itself became increasingly diluted. Today, the conventional meaning still exists and often emerges as I discuss the subject with teachers, students, parents, and others. But it seems to be growing ever fainter, like the trace of a pencil mark that lingers after erasure. Printed boldly over the top of the erasure is a new meaning, distinctly at odds with the traditional notion of reflection: reflection, it proclaims, is a form of action.

And now even that new meaning, imparted by Dewey and Schön, is growing fuzzy. "Reflection," writes John Loughran, a specialist in teacher education and reflective practice, "has developed a variety of meanings as the bandwagon has traveled through the world of [educational] practice."[31] Sure enough, when I come across the word in scholarly and professional texts, it often appears as little more than a slogan, used in conjunction with such trendy and ambiguous terms as "journaling," "heal-ing," "dialoguing," and "closure"—suggesting that reflection is morphing into a solipsistic probing of the inner self that mimics depth of thought: *self*-reflection.

In this way, as it moves out into the popular domain, reflec-tion is fast becoming one of those modular terms deemed by linguist Uwe Pörksen to be "plastic words."[32] These are terms that have become stripped, through overuse, of their precise original meanings; they are used indiscriminately, like Lego blocks, in conjunction with other plastic words, and therefore actually function to inhibit deep thought. Superficial discourse about reflection has become a formulaic, mind-numbing sub-stitute for engaging in the real thing.

The upshot is that we are left with no language with which to talk about reflection in its conventional sense. How likely, then, I wonder, are we to discuss, or even to notice, that the reflection of solitude and slowness is slowly slipping away?

* * *

I said earlier that there are three main ways of responding to the apparent impossibility of reflection in our lives: laughing it off, perceiving evidence of it in diverse activities and modes of thought that would not normally be considered reflective, and redefining it. But of course, there is a fourth response, and that is the province of this book: to reclaim the traditional meaning of the word as a form of deep thought that takes place in conditions of quietude and slowness—as, even more, a mindful, careful way of being in the world—and, having done so, to embark upon a conversation about why it matters.

Chapter 2

WHY DOES REFLECTION MATTER?

WHAT DOES IT MEAN TO BE A THINKING BEING IN THE TWENTY-first century? This is the kind of question that has preoccupied philosophers for centuries. It is particularly difficult to answer now, at a time when thought itself is in the process of being reconceived in computational, utilitarian terms that accord less with human capabilities than with those of our so-called smart machines. The reconceptualization of reflection that I described in the previous chapter is part of this subtle and largely unnoticed shift in how we regard and value our own cognitive processes. Increasingly, deep, slow thought is devalued in favour of the kind of rapid reaction and calculation at which computers excel. (Indeed, in Douglas Adams' *The Hitchhiker's Guide to the Galaxy*, Deep Thought *is* a computer, specially built to determine the answer to the "Ultimate Question about Life, the Universe, and Everything."[1]) At the same time, it is not uncommon to find reflection represented as a dysfunctional mode of thought: from Hamlet to Herzog, the propensity to endless reverie without corresponding action is often a fictional character's tragic flaw.

That said, what, if anything, is reflection good for? In order to answer this question, it is necessary to probe a little deeper into what reflective thought actually entails. What exactly do I mean when I say it is a form of deep thought? What *is* deep thought, and what is the difference between it and superficial thought? Sensory data can offer little help in answering these questions. The person sitting silently in what appears to be serious contemplation may actually be mentally composing a grocery list, while the solitary jogger passing down the street may be in a state of mind more closely approximating what I would call reflective.

My purpose in this chapter is to address such questions and, ultimately, to make a case for why reflection matters. In order to do so, I must elaborate upon the definition offered in the previous chapter, in which I asserted the importance of recovering a conceptualization of reflection as a form of thought that takes place during moments of withdrawal from the social world, and particularly from the chaotic, hyper-stimulating world that many of us now inhabit.

To begin, I want to differentiate reflection from rational thought, which is synonymous with logic and analysis. At the risk of oversimplifying the vast amount that has been written on the subject over the years, I describe rational thought as systematic, calculative, and instrumental: problems are solved and decisions are made based on a careful, step-by-step analysis of facts and empirical data rather than by means of intuition, insight, or emotion. Hence, most dictionaries will offer "sane" as a synonym for rational; indeed, because it is the quality that has long been regarded as distinguishing *Homo sapiens* from other creatures, rationality is also generally considered to be synonymous with humanity. Our species is defined in ancient Greek philosophy as "the rational animal."

Reflection, on the other hand, takes place spontaneously and organically, without the guidance of formula or even necessarily intent. While writing this book, I serendipitously came upon several passages that beautifully evoke the nature of reflection and, more particularly, the unplanned but vital "aha" moments to which periods of reflection can give rise. The first is from the preface to Joseph Conrad's 1907 novel, *The Secret Agent*, in which Conrad describes how his mind began to work with bits of random information that came his way, through conversations and books, and eventually synthesized them into an idea that became the basis for the novel:

> [A]ll of a sudden I felt myself stimulated. And then ensued in my mind what a student of chemistry would best understand from the analogy of the addition of the tiniest little drop of the right kind, precipitating the process of crystallization in a test tube containing some colourless solution.[2]

In the second passage, from *Phenomenology of Perception*, philosopher Maurice Merleau-Ponty similarly describes reflection as a generative form of thought in which "meanings sometimes recombine to form new thought . . . and we are transported to the heart of the matter, we find the source."[3] Finally, in Martin Heidegger's *Discourse on Thinking*, I came upon a line that succinctly describes reflection as thought that "demands of us that we engage ourselves with what at first sight does not go together at all."[4]

What this eclectic selection of passages essentially conveys is a conceptualization of reflection as a mode of thought that entails mulling over ideas that have no necessary connection and eventually producing from them, and from the perceived interconnections among them, new meanings and ideas. Reflection can thus be seen as being more closely aligned with creativity than analysis. This understanding is in fact shared by many of the individuals with whom I have discussed the topic of reflection over the past few years. In conversations with a diverse range of people, I have repeatedly heard reflection described, in terms popularized by Dewey and Schön, as a form of action. But many of the students, teachers, and others with whom I spoke also described reflection in ways that clearly associated it with creation. For some, the connection was explicit: "Reflection is . . . a creative process," said one person, while another agreed: "I think there is a strong link between reflection and creativity." Others spoke more obliquely about reflection as a form of random synthesis, in which apparently unrelated pieces—ideas, events, texts—are brought into conjunction to create something new. Consider the following four examples:

> [Reflection is] a way to move from one place and space in time, to connect it to another place and space in time so it happens more purposefully as opposed to haphazardly or by luck.

> Reflection, it's not letting my mind go around whatever. It's really focusing on something, but letting my mind go within that focus at the same time . . . I'm totally immersed in thinking about that and taking all these discrepant pieces that are making no sense to me, and I'm trying to bring sense to them.

> [Reflection happens] especially when you strike authors or come across articles that align with your thinking, and you're questioning and you're thinking, "let's take a listen in on their writing and their thinking"—their reflection,

I guess. And how does it resonate with you, and does it resonate, and does it fit?

Okay, so I have an awareness of that, now where else can I go? Where will this lead me now? Okay, so that fits with that, so, all right, now I'm going to go over there.

What can we extract from this collection of descriptions from teachers and students, novelists and philosophers? Reflection would seem to be a dynamic, non-linear mode of thought in which the mind assimilates random bits of material that have been gathered serendipitously, from readings, conversations, and experiences. The mind recombines these pieces and, in conditions of silence and withdrawal, spontaneously and unexpectedly produces a flash of insight, an entirely new idea or way of thinking about something. Reflection is therefore "deep" in the sense that it probes below the level of the known and the obvious to discover new, elusive ideas and perspectives. It is also, in that sense, fundamentally creative—and that is a first answer to the question of why reflection matters.

* * *

In placing reflection squarely within the domain of creativity as opposed to logic and analysis, I am defining the word quite differently from Dewey, who presents reflection as a step-by-step scientific process that clearly falls within the province of rational thought. Science can be defined as the systemization of knowledge and its acquisition. In order to better understand phenomena, scientists generally follow explicit processes to dismantle those phenomena into discrete, more easily analyzable pieces. The result, of course, is that the vast, mysterious world has become a comprehensible, manageable sphere, in which both scientific knowledge and technological innovation flourish. But despite its normative power within our society, science can only tell us so much, particularly when it comes to understanding ourselves and the world we live in.

In *The Pentagon of Power*, Lewis Mumford illustrates the limitations of this reductive frame of mind by asking us to imagine that clocks do not exist—and that one has just fallen from the sky.[5] Having never before seen a clock, and knowing nothing of its history or function, our scientists would immediately begin to dismantle it and measure, photograph, and analyse in careful detail its face, hands, springs, wheels, and other parts. But the accurate, detailed reports of physicists, chemists, metallurgists, and other specialists would bring us no closer to an understanding of what the clock *is*. In fact, says Mumford, amidst all this dissection and analysis, the clock itself would simply disappear.

Despite the limits of analytical thought, ours is a culture that considers the processes and products of science to be the primary source of knowledge and truth. Increasingly, we are unwilling to heed reflective insights unless they are backed by purportedly objective study, empirical data, and quantification. Without such backing, the most sober analyses are likely to be dismissed, while outrageous claims will tend to be accepted uncritically, provided they have the weight of science and numbers behind them. As Neil Postman observes in *Technopoly*, "it is possible to say almost anything without contradiction provided you begin your utterance with the words 'A study has shown...' or 'Scientists now tell us that...'"[6] Both Postman and Mumford stress that this over-valuation of scientific thought, and the concomitant under-valuation of reflection, creates an unhealthy social imbalance.

In co-opting reflection to describe scientific process, then, Dewey and his followers were implicitly privileging the technical mindset while devaluing non-scientific forms of mental activity, which were dismissed as random, purposeless, and chaotic. As a result, reflection in its conventional sense—the reflection that takes place in conditions of solitude and slowness—fell further out of favour, while more and more value was placed upon analytical thought, instrumental action, and a capability for superficial, rapid reaction.

One of the clear consequences of this devaluation of reflection is that it becomes necessary to ask, Why does reflection matter? We never feel that it is necessary to pose a similar question about scientific thinking, for the products of science surround us, while reflection, to judge from the lack of immediate, tangible results, would seem to be time ill spent. That is why reflection is also known as "woolgathering." The term has its origins in the Middle Ages, when young children would sometimes gather tufts of wool snagged on bushes and hedges from passing sheep. The amounts of wool that could be collected in this manner were so negligible that it was considered a waste of time, as fruitless and unprofitable as the purposeless reveries that the word eventually came to signify.

* * *

So what does woolgathering yield? I have suggested that reflection is generative, but what exactly is created if nothing tangible is produced? By way of answering this question, I turn once again to Lewis Mumford, whose thought experiment I described above. Born in 1895, Mumford was a brilliant autodidact whose many works include influential studies of urban planning, American literature, architecture, art, and technological development. Mumford grew up in New York City during a period when scientific and technological innovation flourished, personified by the astounding achievements of such renowned inventors as Edison, Marconi, and the Wright brothers. In his autobiography, Mumford recalls an episode in high school that vividly captures the sense of wonder and endless possibility that science evoked in those days: "Yes: it was in 1911, I remember, that my physics teacher held up his pencil and said: 'If we knew how to unlock the energy in this carbon, a few pencils would be enough to run the subways of New York.'"[7]

Although the young Mumford shared this enthusiasm for the possibilities offered by scientific advances, he became increasingly troubled over the years by the implications for humanity of a widespread passion for mechanistic, analytical thought, without a concomitant valuation of the subjective realm of emotion and creativity. In a talk given to Radcliffe College's graduating class of 1956, he emphasized the importance of reflection, encouraging the young men and women he addressed to balance social engagement with "seasons of withdrawal and solitude."[8] Mumford then went on to express his conviction that such moments of contemplation are essential to our very humanity: without them, he feared, we will allow ourselves to become increasingly overwhelmed by the dictates of ceaseless technological advancement, leaving "the very core of our life to become hollow and dismally empty."[9]

I have chosen to focus on Mumford not only because he has much to say about the importance of reflection, but because his work in general bears all the hallmarks of reflective thought, as I define it. First, his thinking is not analytic and linear but synthetic and holistic. Throughout his working life, he actively resisted the social pressures that would have had him retreat into and further buttress silos of specialization. Mumford was stubbornly interdisciplinary, and he knew that this would allow him to make connections that were unavailable to someone whose perspective was constrained by the boundaries of a single field of study. As he writes in *Technics and Civilization*, "our intellectual interests are already so specialized that we habitually begin our thinking with abstractions and fragments which are as difficult to unify by the methods of specialism as were the broken pieces of Humpty-Dumpty after he had fallen off the wall."[10] A self-proclaimed generalist, but certainly no dilettante, Mumford devoted a lifetime of intellectual labour to the synthesis of ideas from many areas of inquiry into entirely original thought.

This ability to draw deep connections between often disparate fields and sources is, in my view, a clear sign of the reflective mind at work. When a student speaks to me intelligently about the key points in a lecture or assigned reading, I am pleased because I know that he has comprehended the material. When, far more rarely, a student stumblingly tries to articulate her awareness of the ways in which two or three disparate readings and discussions spark off each other, igniting new possibilities in her mind, I am delighted, because I know that she has entered the dimension of original thought and insight that I call reflection. Literary critic and essayist Sven Birkerts clarifies this distinction between comprehension and reflective insight:

> It is one thing to absorb a fact, to situate it alongside other facts in a configuration, and quite another to contemplate that fact at leisure, allowing it to declare its connection with other facts, its thematic destiny, its resonance.[11]

A second characteristic of Mumford's reflections that distinguishes them from scientific thinking is his willingness to engage with subjective, non-empirical ways of knowing: intuitions, feelings, and beliefs. Certainly, Mumford insists upon the importance of going out and observing the world. Many of his insights are based upon the hours he spent walking the streets of New York, taking keen note of people, structures, and the movements of traffic. But the material from which Mumford's reflective insights are stitched come as much from the invisible world of myths, dreams, and values—his own, as well as those of the civilizations he studied—as it does from observation. Scientists, of course, must operate within this subjective realm, but they distance themselves from it as much as possible by basing their conclusions upon evidence emerging from controlled experiments that can be precisely replicated. The reflective intellect does not reject the empirical, but neither is it limited to working with verifiable data.

Consider, for example, Mumford's intriguing speculations about how the pyramids were built in the absence of the kinds of technologies that would be used today to move massive stones into place. Mumford suggests that, during the long period of cultural preparation for mechanization and industrialization, ancient kings learned to coordinate the effort of hundreds, even thousands, of slaves and servants, who were forced to put aside their individuality in the shared cause of erecting pyramids and other massive monuments to kingly power. Compelled to work together toward a single purpose, the king's subjects formed what Mumford called a "megamachine."[12] No scientist ever dismantled a megamachine for analysis because a megamachine cannot exist independently of the human beings and social relations of which it is composed; it can therefore only be reconstructed by a reflective mind willing to weave together myth and the dreamworld, historical fact and conjecture. Because it is not tied to the world of empirical data, reflection is a potentially rich source of insight.

A third way in which Mumford's speculations are typical of reflective thought is that they are provisional, not absolute. The scientist undertakes orderly, empirical investigations with the explicit purpose of producing objective, generalizable truths about the world of things—for example, how the brain works or how algae reproduce. "In scientific training," observes mathematician and philosopher Alfred North Whitehead, "the first thing to do with an idea is to prove it."[13] Reflection, on the other hand, is not a planned, systematic process producing certitude but a habit of mind, a natural inclination to engage deeply with ideas and to discover new, and often unexpected, connections between them. The reflective mind veers from the linear road and follows its own inclinations. As Heidegger puts it, "The ways of reflection constantly change, ever according to the way at which a path begins, ever according to the portion of the way that it traverses, ever according to the distant view that opens along the way."[14] The soundness of the connections made during this meandering journey may be tested with thought experiments (such as imaginary clocks falling from the sky), but the reflective intellect is far less concerned with proving the truth of its speculations than with provoking further contemplation. Proof, after all, produces certainty, which tends to harden into a fixed world view; and a fixed world view is inherently antithetical to reflection. Science's absolutes and certainties provide us with a stable ground from which to view the world, but scientific thinking, which seeks the closure of truth, could not have led Mumford to his highly original insights about megamachines. Those insights were available only through reflection, which entails a perennial openness to provisional truths, a willingness to forego order and method, and an eagerness to consider the serendipitous possibilities that emerge as ideas are cross-fertilized by the random flitting of the reflective mind.

Finally, Mumford's work is characteristic of reflective thought in that, although it was not intended to produce immediate, tangible results, it was oriented to social change. For reflection, as one commentator contends, is essentially political, insofar as it "either hastens or defers the realization of a more rational, just, and fulfilling society."[15] When we reflect, we ultimately construct not only new perspectives and ideas but also new ways of being in the world. The significance of Mumford's megamachine transcends ancient history, for surely the megamachine persists today in such collective forces as armies, bureaucracies, and assembly lines. Further, the megamachine gave rise to the perception of work as a source of power, something that could be harnessed by reducing human beings to mechanical units required to perform standardized, precise, and endlessly repeatable tasks. Indeed, we can attribute to the megamachine the fundamental paradox of a humanity that is capable of accomplishments that attest to the greatness of the human spirit— carving canals through mountains of solid rock, building walls and roadways spanning hundreds of miles of difficult terrain, damming and diverting rushing rivers, constructing vast temples and skyscrapers—that can only be achieved by reducing individuals to mere mechanical elements compelled to perform a limited task through repetitive and highly standardized activities. In offering the concept of the megamachine, Mumford is ultimately attempting to forge the way to a shared vision of a more balanced social world that gives equal precedence to the rational and reflective aspects of our being.

* * *

Reflection, we can see, is more than mere woolgathering. Contemplations that take place in retreat from the social world may very well lead to a revisioning of that world, and that revisioning may precipitate action. What I am suggesting is a new relationship between reflection and action that does not appear to be adequately represented by either of the two models offered by Schön. The first, *reflection-in-action* (reflection and action occurring simultaneously), is, as I suggested in the previous chapter, an oxymoron: if true reflection requires solitude and slowness, then it simply cannot take place in the midst of action. The second, *reflection-on-action* (action first, then reflection about it), also fails to approximate what I have in mind, although it has become a common practice in classrooms based upon the belief that teaching and learning experiences should be consolidated through discussion, evaluation, and other activities. But to refer to such practices as reflection—and not, more accurately, as review or assessment—is a misnomer; it suggests that reflection is merely a recollection, reconsideration, and evaluation of a learning experience that is tacked on to the end of a lesson and that may, when time is short, be foregone without much consequence.

Given the inadequacy of these two models, I want to posit a third possible relationship between action and reflection, *reflection-then-action*, in which reflection comes first and informs subsequent action. I believe that this is the only relationship between action and reflection that is worth considering. While we should value silent moments of contemplation, insofar as they nourish and sustain the human spirit, the reverberations of these reflective moments are most deeply felt in subsequent actions, undertaken mindfully, with care and forethought.

I believe that action informed by reflection is likely to enhance civic capacity and social justice; however, it is important to clarify that I do not characterize "action," in this context, as a dramatic exploit that rocks the foundations of society. Here, it perhaps becomes necessary to differentiate reflection from another form of rational thought: critical thinking. Reflection, as I have suggested, entails a creative synthesis of discrepant elements; critical thinking, conversely, is analytical. Further, reflection is best characterized as a habit of mind, even a way of being, while critical thinking is typically described in textbooks in terms of "skills," "tools," and "processes" that can be imparted to students. These skills, tools, and processes are considered especially important given the ocean of information that students confront when they go online; the general belief is that individuals who develop critical thinking skills will be better equipped to deal with this onslaught of data. In particular, they will have become aware of the ways in which websites, advertisements, and other texts attempt to manipulate and persuade, as well as adept at using logic and reason to refute and defuse such arguments and inducements. Peter McLaren, a leading voice on the topic of critical thinking and critical pedagogy, characterizes critical thinking as "a *pedagogical negativism*—to doubt everything."[16] While important, this kind of learned skepticism is quite different from reflection, a form of thinking that is concomitant with openness and synthesis—with putting things together rather than deconstructing them.

But the difference goes deeper. Critical thinking thrives in a progress-obsessed, reactive culture in which we are continually exhorted to "embrace change" as inherently progressive. Thus, moving forward is inextricably associated with radical structural changes and quick fixes: the overthrowing of ideological and political regimes, sweeping educational reforms, revolutionary technological solutions, and even radical surgical procedures that change everything. In order to advance in this culture, the critical thinker seizes hold of the inadequacies of current ideas and practices and severs relations with them in order to enact change. Critical thinking, then, is intended to produce a severe and irreparable break from tradition, a break that must lead to a period of personal and social upheaval, as new ideas and practices emerge to take the place of those that have been rejected.

Reflection, on the other hand, is about lingering, looking both forward and back with mindfulness and care. It is not about resisting change—social change and innovation are inevitably stimulated by the new ideas to which reflection gives rise—but about slowing its pace, giving us the time to understand what a given change means, to decide if it is really in our best interests, and if it is, how we might best go about it in an orderly, peaceful way that upholds those values and practices that are worth preserving. Reflective change happens within continuity rather than because of a revolutionary upheaval or drastic break; it therefore tends to promote social and personal stability rather than the constant state of instability that goes hand-in-hand with critical thinking.

Reflection-then-action may give rise to small, everyday initiatives and undertakings that, in their cumulative effect, restore personal and social balance, perspective, and mindfulness, thus creating more space for reflection. It might, for example, find expression in reading or writing, artistic endeavours or social interactions; but it might also be followed by actions that appear, to a world hell-bent on change and forward motion, to be non-actions. These actions could include deliberately slowing or pausing the frenzied activity of everyday life, or finding a way, amidst the constant stimulation and the hum of technological devices, to carve out a moment of silence. While such moments may be considered "lost" time, in the sense that required work is not being done or required curriculum outcomes are not being checked off, only within the uncharted space of silence is it possible to fully synthesize the daily onslaught of information, and perhaps generate from it new questions and new possibilities.

The actions that emerge from reflection might seem small or even mundane, but they are precisely the kinds of actions that most of us are capable of making in our day-to-day lives, and their potential cumulative power should not be underestimated. As Mumford observes, "Choice manifests itself in society in small increments and moment-to-moment decisions as well as in loud dramatic struggles."[17]

Of course, while critical thinking has emerged in recent years as an educational mantra that appears in almost all curricular documents, reflection as a slow, silent mode of thought is in retreat. Isolated thought is often characterized as antithetical to social reality and therefore contrary to the needs and interests of the community. However, perhaps as we consider what it means to live in a society in which many important actions are undertaken without prior reflection, we can begin to perceive the falseness of this dichotomy. Reflection-then-action is a vital corrective to the increasing prevalence of ill-considered actions carried out for self-serving purposes, for immediate gratification, or in narrow response to the dictates of accountability and quantification. Making time for reflection-then-action in classrooms, workplaces, and elsewhere expresses a commitment to slow, silent thought as a way of deepening our engagement with the world. Here, then, is a second answer to the question of why reflection matters.

* * *

Having taken pains to distinguish reflection from rational modes of thought such as science and critical thinking, I now must acknowledge that, like most dichotomies, this one is not entirely tenable. In emphasizing the distinction between reflection and science, I have drawn upon a representation of the scientific process that is more stereotypical than real. The public understanding of science, which arose in part to buttress boundaries between rational, purposeful intellectual processes and contemplative thought, is very much tied up with the hackneyed image of the white-coated scientist working in a laboratory, mixing chemicals or using a microscope to gaze at molecular structures. In this chapter, I have intentionally activated that stereotype in order to reinforce the boundary between the two modes of thought for the opposite purpose: to assert the value of reverie over scientific thinking. Furthermore, I have deliberately misrepresented science in order to give reflection the privileged position that science usually holds in public discourse and thought. In practice, scientists spend much of their time in retreat and in reflection: the laboratory is a site not only for experiments but for precisely the kind of withdrawal from the world that I described in Chapter 1.[18] And the deep, generative thought described in this chapter is most certainly a primary source of insight and new ideas, even in a realm that purports to be entirely rational.

Similarly, critical thinking cannot be as cleanly severed from reflection as I have suggested. I am quite aware, for example, that my own reflections on reflection in this book began with a sensitivity to the mis- and overuse of language—the kind of probing into semantic distortions and ambiguities that is supposed to be the province of critical thinking. The inseparable link between critical thinking and reflection is particularly evident when critical thought is directed toward social relationships and merges with critical *theory*, grounded in Marxist, feminist, and poststructuralist perspectives. I cannot imagine the work of esteemed critical thinkers such as Henry Giroux, Paulo Freire, and bell hooks, who strive to overturn existing assumptions about teaching and learning in our society, beginning in any way but with independent thought in conditions of silence and withdrawal. Nor can I imagine asking a student of any age to be *critical* without expecting that they will also be *reflective*, for any attempt to deconstruct a term or concept is best undertaken in light of a contemplation of its meaning and resonances. In fact, critical thought and reflection are so intertwined in practice that they have given rise to an apparent oxymoron: "critical reflection," a term that merges generative, independent thought with analytic processes aimed at dismantling discourses and deconstructing praxis.

Acknowledging that the boundaries between rational and reflective thought are not absolute does not undermine my attempts to show that reflection matters. Rather, it discloses the vital role that reflection plays, or should play, in just about every aspect of our intellectual lives, even those processes and discourses, such as science and critical thinking, that exist by virtue of a purposeful exclusion of reflective ways of knowing. Rationality has long been identified as the characteristic that distinguishes human beings from the rest of the animal kingdom, but surely reflectivity—the propensity to stop and think—also sets us apart, and is an equally ineluctable part of who we are: we are rational *and* reflective animals. Indeed, asking why reflection matters leads inevitably to the question of who we would be without reflection. What would it mean to be human in a milieu in which people never paused in their daily rounds to contemplate, to connect ideas, and thus to conceive new possibilities for themselves and their world? One young man to whom I posed this question inadvertently echoed both Mumford and poet T.S. Eliot when he replied, "Without reflection, it's almost like we're hollow." Can it be that, in renouncing silent reverie, we lose something of ourselves, something fundamental?

That is precisely the message that underlies much of Lewis Mumford's work, and it is the message I have sought to convey throughout this chapter by placing rational thought in the subordinate position that reflection normally holds in our society. We cannot simply reject one aspect of our being and allow another to gain precedence in everything we do without creating a severe personal and social disequilibrium. It is only by opening ourselves to reflection, according it value as a way of thinking and being, that we can counteract the prevailing influence of the technical mindset, with its privileging of efficiency and instrumentalism, and thus achieve balance and fulfillment in our lives. That is the final answer to the question of why reflection matters.

* * *

This conclusion, however, points the way to another question: Just how did reflection become a vital part of the human makeup? How, in other words, did human beings develop a capacity and a propensity for reflection? That is the question I take up in the next chapter.

Chapter 3

THE RISE OF THE REFLECTIVE MIND

To this point I have reclaimed the dwindling concept of reflection as generative thought that takes place in conditions of solitude and slowness, and I have made a case for why reflection, in this sense of the word, matters. In this chapter, I break from the trajectory established in the first two chapters by moving backwards in time. My primary purpose here is to trace the rise of the reflective mind and to consider the role that technology has played in its emergence. A key premise underlying this chapter, and this book as a whole, is that the emergence of new communications technologies changes not only how we interact with one another but ultimately how we think. In a later chapter, I will turn to a consideration of the high-tech devices that are typically called to mind by the word "technology," but here I am using the word more generally, to denote any tool or technique that gives rise to changes in human interactions. As I will show in this chapter, the communications technologies that played an important role in the rise of reflection were the alphabet and the printing press—and even before that, language itself.

Philosophers, anthropologists, neurobiologists, psychologists, and linguists continue to debate which came first, language or thought. Few, however, would dispute the integral relationship between the two—so integral that it is probably most accurate to say that speech and the human mind co-evolved. And just as *Homo sapiens*' development of the capacity for thought was inextricably linked to our species' development of the capacity for spoken language, so, according to many scholars and commentators, was the emergence of reflection concomitant with the development of *written* language.

To begin to reconstruct that historical emergence we must try to cast ourselves back into that ancient world in which the only mode of communication was spoken sounds and accompanying facial expressions and gestures—a difficult, if not impossible, task for those of us enmeshed within a web of written language. Having lived our lives within that matrix of understanding, we have no difficulty conceiving the possibility of capturing language and pinning it to the page—in fact, we do it ourselves every day as we bang out hasty emails or jot reminders on Post-it Notes. But the world we must imagine was one in which words could not be separated from the speaker: they were made with the speaker's breath, and were as transitory and evanescent as that breath, each vanishing immediately as the next word was spoken. Language was conceived of as an event; there was no concept of words as *things*, as separable grammatical units.

Communication in this oral culture was comprised chiefly of sounds, each of which had an agreed-upon meaning within the context of a particular group. Many of these word-sounds would have been related to practical goals, such as organizing cooperative food-gathering efforts; many of them would have been chanted or sung during communal gatherings in order to perpetuate knowledge and lore. There was no other way to preserve and pass on such knowledge except through the shared ritual utterances of members of the tribe. Like most people today I usually turn to a book or, more and more often, the Internet when I am seeking particular information. But the idea of an individual accessing information, regardless of the medium, would have made absolutely no sense to these people. To them, knowledge had no independent existence from the knower; it was a function of the group, created and perpetuated within ritualized exchanges.

Media guru Marshall McLuhan refers to the psychological world in which people with only spoken language live as "acoustic space," which he describes as "boundless, directionless, horizonless, in the dark of the mind, in the world of emotion, by primordial intuition, by terror."[1] The finest literary depiction of this highly charged acoustic space is the storm-struck heath in which the mad, anguished King Lear wanders, "look[ing] with [his] ears."[2] I gain an appreciation for the holistic, emotionally charged nature of acoustic space when I attend music recitals and concerts. When I *watch* a performance, my eyes roaming from pianist to guitarist to cellist, what I tend to hear are separate instruments: piano, guitar, cello. But when I close my eyes and just *listen*, what I experience is one enveloping sound. Others may experience the same contrast between immersion and separation by listening to a hockey or baseball game on the radio and then watching it on television, or by watching a battle scene on a DVD, then replaying it, closing their eyes, and just listening to the same scene. To hear the game or the battle scene, as opposed to seeing it, is to experience it in a different way—to become more immersed and emotionally involved. Open your eyes, and you withdraw from that noisy, heated realm.

* * *

The first major step in the development of written language was the emergence of numbers. Thanks to the work of Denise

Schmandt-Besserat, an archeologist specializing in the art and artifacts of the ancient Middle East, we can be fairly certain that numbers originated with the need to keep accounts of agricultural and, later, man-made goods. Based upon an analysis of her archeological discoveries, Schmandt-Besserat theorizes that agricultural activity in the Fertile Crescent (the area of the Middle East that now includes all or parts of Iran, Iraq, Israel, Jordan, Lebanon, and Syria) gave rise to a new economy based upon the hoarding of agricultural surpluses.[3] In times of plenty, farmers were expected to surrender their surplus crops to temple leaders, who in turn were responsible for storing and redistributing the goods in times of need.

In order for this redistribution economy to function, an accurate method of record keeping was required, and so, around 8000 BC, a token-based system of accounting emerged. The tokens were small clay objects whose shape roughly approximated the goods they stood for or the containers in which those goods were usually transported. For example, a sheaf of grain was represented by a small clay cone, while oil was represented by an oval token, similar in shape to the jars in which oil was carried. These tokens were used in a system of one-to-one correspondence: for example, the temple accountants would need five separate oval tokens in order to represent five jars of oil.

The method that developed for keeping accounts involved putting the tokens for each transaction in a separate hollow clay ball, which was then sealed shut. The sealed ball was tamper-proof, but it was also opaque; in order to see what was inside the temple accountants had to break the clay ball open. Over time, they began to realize that they could overcome this difficulty by impressing upon the outside of the clay ball an indication of its contents, using the same representational system as the tokens:

one oval for one jar of oil, three cones for three measures of grain, and so forth. And once they had taken that step, it was only a matter of time before they arrived at the realization that they did not need the tokens at all: the symbols themselves, impressed or inscribed on clay tablets, would do. Schmandt-Besserat declares that the first tablets, created around 3500 BC, "were a decisive step in the invention of writing and amounted to a revolution in communication technology."[4]

One way to gain some insight into the nature of the intellectual shift involved is to look at it in terms of the stages of cognitive development identified by Jean Piaget. Piaget was a Swiss biologist and psychologist who is perhaps best known for identifying four main stages through which children progress as they develop intellectual skills. He labelled those stages sensorimotor, preoperational thinking, concrete operations, and formal operations. According to Piaget, at about the age of seven a modern-day child typically moves into the preoperational thinking stage, which entails the ability to work with symbols. At this point, the child no longer needs to use manipulatives, such as blocks, or count pictures of objects, such as apples, in order to solve addition problems: he or she is able to solve a problem using the numerals alone.

Correctly or not, Piaget believed that these four stages of individual cognitive development mimic the cognitive evolution of our species as a whole. Certainly the transition to preoperational thinking is something like the transformation experienced, on a very large scale, when people moved from a three-dimensional, token-based system to a two-dimensional, symbol-based method of recording accounts. However, to our forbears, the momentousness of this transition was heightened by the additional realization (something that every seven-year-old today already takes for granted) that, in their new symbolic, two-dimensional form, word-sounds could be inscribed in clay, cowhide, or parchment, where they could exist independently of people.

Each token or sign inscribed on the outside of a clay ball represented both a number and a thing. As indicated above, one cone stood for one measure of grain, while one oval shape stood for one jar of oil. However, Schmandt-Besserat's archaeological findings suggest that over time another important development took place: the number and the thing began to split apart. Eventually, two sets of signs emerged: signs that indicated number, regardless of the thing being counted, and signs that indicated the thing being counted, regardless of how many there were. (This development would correspond with Piaget's formal operations stage, in which the child at approximately age 12 develops the capability for abstract thought.) Now it was no longer necessary to draw five ovals to represent five jars of oil. Instead, all that was needed were two signs: a sign for "five" and a sign for "jar of oil." In this way, numerals came into existence.

Written language followed in due course. At first, it was composed largely of ideograms, pictorial characters that represented, in stylized form, something concrete, such as the simplified oval representation of a jar of oil. Ideograms were linked to a specific meaning, but the sound that the ideogram invoked was arbitrary and, if the ideogram happened to be used by several groups with different dialects, would very likely differ from place to place. Moreover, since there was a separate ideogram for every thing and every idea, the system was unwieldy. Few people were able to undergo the lengthy process of tutelage required to become literate, and even for the initiated it would have been a challenge to remember thousands of separate ideograms. Further, while ideograms were effective for recording goods and amounts, it was not always easy to use them to record the names of those who contributed the goods.

These factors may have provided incentive for the development of syllabaries, systems that attempted to bind written symbols not to particular meanings, such as "jar of oil," but to the individual sound-units, or syllables, in a spoken language. The closest thing we have to syllabaries today is rebus word puzzles, in which the sounds of words are represented by pictures of things. For example, the name Tony might be represented by the picture of a toe followed by the picture of a knee ("toe-knee"). However, not all names are equally amenable to visual representation. For instance, you would need recourse to the alphabet in order to represent the name Jake, with a picture of a blue jay followed by the letter K. And many other names, from Ann to Zachary, defy visual representation entirely.

Syllabary systems therefore met with little success and were eventually usurped by the *aleph-beth*, a consonant-based system developed by northern Semitic tribes around 1500 BC. Whereas ideograms had depicted things and syllabaries syllables, this Semitic innovation used only 22 consonants to graphically represent all the discrete sounds of which human spoken language in that place and time was comprised. When the Greeks appropriated this system some seven centuries later, they dropped several of the consonants, added vowels, and renamed it *alpha-beta*. And thus our phonetic alphabet, a system of 26 arbitrary signs (more or less in some languages, such as German and Irish) that stand for sounds rather than things, came into being. Other alphabets, such as the Cyrillic, used primarily in Russia and Eastern Europe, have different stories of origin, but their effects were similarly transformational.

* * *

It is difficult for us to appreciate the full significance and impact of an alphabet composed of arbitrary, abstract symbols. We live in an information environment in which signs that bear no concrete relationship to what they represent confront us at every turn. In fact, almost every activity in which we engage, from looking at the alarm clock first thing in the morning to driving home at the end of the workday, involves negotiating such signs. Unlike people living in an acoustic space where spoken language is always addressed by one living person to another, we have internalized an understanding that the word can be transformed from an immediate sound to an arbitrary, abstract visual symbol and, in the process, separated from both the speaker and the living present.

What kinds of changes, in particular, did the invention and spread of written language eventually wreak upon the thought-world of ancient peoples? First, as I have already suggested, there was the tremendous psychological impact of being able to freeze human thought, so to speak—to transform it from an evanescent sound to a more or less permanent *thing* available for scrutiny. In *The Spell of the Sensuous*, ecologist and philosopher David Abram sums up the implications of this seismic shift in ways of thinking and knowing:

> In contact with the written word, a new, apparently autonomous, sensibility merges into experience, a new self that can enter into relation with its own verbal traces, can view and ponder its own statements even as it formulates them, and can thus reflexively interact with itself in isolation from other persons and from the surrounding animate earth.[5]

When hitherto fleeting ideas could be captured and rendered visible, it began to matter who the ideas had come from. And it became possible to conceive of oneself as an individual, possessing an identity formed not only through one's interrelationships with other people but by an engagement with ideas that took place outside the social realm.

Equally significant was the fact that alphabetic writing and reading created the possibility of achieving a distance from the emotional lifeworld in which, up to this point, all communication had taken place. Acoustic space was highly involving, but as people began to communicate more and more with the written word, their eyes took over. The alphabet thus ushered humanity into a radically altered information environment, a visual space in which people were predisposed to stand apart from the fray. As Edmund Carpenter, an anthropologist who studied the effects of new media in tribal cultures, puts it, "Sight has a natural bias toward detachment, creating the detached observer, whereas sound has an opposite bias: it surrounds, involves—one steps into it."[6]

To return to an earlier analogy, people in a society newly exposed to written language might be compared to members of an audience who open their eyes during a performance of orchestral music, only to find their perception altered. Rather than experiencing the music viscerally as a single embracing sound, they find themselves attending somewhat dispassionately, and as if from a new distance, to its separate elements, perhaps appreciating the virtuosity of the violinist or the syncopation of the drums. In a visual space brought into being by the fragmentation of the haptic world of sound into the orderly alphabet, everything was newly susceptible to just such an objective analysis. Even the most amorphous of concepts, like time itself, could now be captured and pinned down, its orderly dissection visually represented by the calendar and the clock.

In opening up possibilities for a new way of thinking that we would now call rational, objective, and analytic, the alphabet was a precondition for the rise of science. But it also paved the way for speculative thought—the stuff of both literature and science. In part, the rise of speculative thinking had to do with the fact that, having been relieved by writing from the burden of memorization, the mind was free for the first time to indulge in contemplation of diverse and future possibilities. I experience a similar liberation when, having written down an unfamiliar phone number, I am able to stop reciting the phone number over and over and start actually thinking about what I want to say in the forthcoming conversation.

But there was another important reason why writing fostered speculative thought. Spoken language was used to communicate about concrete, immediate things and actual events. Even at its most fanciful, it was used to create stories and myths that would explain real events in the natural world: "Thunder and lightning are caused when Zeus hurls his thunderbolt. A volcano erupts because a terrible creature is imprisoned in the mountain and every now and then struggles to get free."[7] People in oral cultures rarely consider possibilities beyond the world of experience, beyond what Walter Ong, author of *Orality and Literacy*, calls "the human lifeworld,"[8] because their language simply does not allow for it; indeed, many tribal languages still in existence actually lack a future tense. It was therefore difficult if not impossible for our ancestors to frame "what if?" questions, let alone to posit answers to such questions. This tendency to focus on the concrete persisted even when people began using written ideograms. Ideograms, after all, were equally grounded in the real: a picture will not communicate anything to people who have not seen or experienced the thing that it is meant to represent. True, ideograms were used to write down stories, but only those that were already very familiar as oft-told oral tales; they were mnemonic devices, not symbols that could be used to create entirely new narratives about unknown people, places, and events.

The alphabet, however, was a mode of communication based on abstract symbols, symbols disconnected from the lifeworld. Because it allowed people to speculate, and to communicate their dreams and fantasies as well as their actual experiences, the alphabet provided a stimulus for inventive and imaginative thinking. (Of course, in expanding the possibilities of human thought and communication beyond the actual, the alphabet also paved the way for another creative use of language: duplicity.)

While writing gave rise to two new modes of thought, the scientific and the speculative, it would take another development, the invention of the printing press, to make possible and prevalent the kind of deep thought that I have called reflection.

* * *

Revolutionary as the consequences of the phonetic alphabet were, these changes in human habits of mind took place very gradually. As the alphabet travelled out of the Middle East into Greece and the rest of Europe, the ability to read and write became associated with social power. Literacy therefore remained for many centuries the province of the very wealthy and members of the ecclesiastical elite, who were responsible for hand copying and preserving manuscripts (most of them religious) for posterity. Until the fifteenth century, most people continued to live in a largely oral information environment, communicating chiefly by means of utterances spoken and heard. But many of those utterances—including sermons, political speeches, public orations, and poetry readings—were now read aloud from written texts; therefore, even if the ability to read and write was limited to a few, most people now understood the concept. The certainties of the medieval thought-world had been irreversibly shaken by the new awareness that it was possible to use abstract symbols to capture and preserve knowledge.

This was the environment into which the printing press was introduced in the mid-fifteenth century. Across Europe, a number of people were experimenting with the possibility of automating the laborious process of copying manuscripts. However, credit for the invention of the printing press is generally given to Johannes Gutenberg, a goldsmith and gem-cutter who lived in the German city of Mainz. Gutenberg designed his press around the principle of movable type, which had actually been invented some 400 years earlier in China. There, the popularity of the innovation had been severely constrained by the inherent difficulties of creating separate type blocks for each of the thousands of Chinese ideograms. However, the principle was ideally suited to a symbol system consisting of only 20 or 30 distinct characters. Gutenberg achieved success by combining movable type with a specially formulated ink and a frame ingeniously modified from a wine press, hence the name, printing press.

The first book to roll off Gutenberg's press, some time around 1450, was a Latin Bible, and from there the printing press and its products proliferated exponentially. Within a few decades, printers' workshops flourished throughout Europe; their products, written increasingly in the vernacular, gave rise to a reading public. By 1550, millions of books had been printed, distributed, and read—more than all the scribes in all the monasteries across Europe would have been able to produce during several centuries of exacting labour. By 1620, philosopher and scientist Francis Bacon was able to observe that print, along with gunpowder and the compass, had already "changed the appearance and state of the whole world."[9]

Once again, the changes wrought by the advent of typography were profound, giving rise to a Europe characterized by radically transformed social organizations, belief systems, and world views. As sociologist David Riesman puts it, once printed books made an appearance, the world could "never be quite the same again—books are, so to speak, the gunpowder of the mind."[10] In her groundbreaking study of the social ramifications of print, *The Printing Press as an Agent of Change*, Elizabeth Eisenstein agrees that Gutenberg's invention had a "cataclysmic effect" on medieval European society.[11] According to Eisenstein, the mass production and distribution of books written in the vernacular was a decisive factor in the decline of the medieval church and the Protestant Reformation, the rise of capitalism and the Industrial Revolution, the flowering of scholarship and scientific publication, and the resulting Copernican revolution. The new capability for mass distribution of an individual's words also gave rise to authorship, copyright, plagiarism, and other notions and practices that would have been foreign to oral societies. Knowledge, once inseparable from the shared rituals through which it was created and perpetuated, came to be regarded as an artifact that could be abstracted and owned by an individual.

These are all significant developments that would profoundly alter the shape of Western civilization and propel it from the Middle Ages into modernity. But our concern here is with the changes that also occurred at the level of individual consciousness. In particular, it is important for our purposes to understand how print amplified a tendency that had been inaugurated with the alphabet: the tendency of people to encounter and create knowledge in isolation rather than as members of a group. As we have seen, the invention of the alphabet made it possible for an individual to acquire and produce knowledge apart from other members of the social group. Nevertheless, in manuscript culture, reading remained a largely social activity. It was still generally assumed that if one set down words on paper, it was with the express intent of later reading those words aloud before others. Indeed, until the seventh century, when the convention of adding spaces between written words became commonplace, reading aloud was a necessity, the only way to abstract meaning from an otherwise indecipherable string of characters.[12] "There was," observes Ivan Illich, "almost no other way of reading than rehearsing the sentences aloud, and listening to hear whether they made sense."[13] A passage in Saint Augustine's *Confessions* illuminates just how foreign the idea of reading to oneself seemed in the fourth century AD. Augustine relates his surprise at encountering Ambrose, the Bishop of Milan, in silent contemplation of a text. "When he was reading," Augustine marvels, "his eyes glided over the pages, and his heart searched out the sense, but his voice and tongue were at rest." The most plausible explanation Augustine can reach for this strange behaviour is that Ambrose is trying to preserve his voice.[14]

Anyone who has ever read a storybook to a group of kindergartners, or watched someone else do so, will have some idea of what reading aloud might have entailed in the early Middle Ages. During story time young children tend to participate quite energetically, clapping, chanting choruses or speaking familiar lines, responding to the teacher's questions, predicting story events, loudly debating characters' motivations, and so forth. And just as pictures play an important role in the child's encounter with the written story, so too did the colourful and often fanciful illuminations in medieval manuscripts give the words additional life and emotional force.[15] In making this comparison, I do not mean to suggest that early medievals were childlike; only that, being relatively new to printed text, they were no more able than kindergarten children to transition directly from the ritualized communal activities in which most oral communications were grounded to silent, solitary reading.

Typography eventually changed all that. Because printed books were more readily available and more portable than manuscripts had ever been, they could easily be carried away to isolated areas, where individuals could quietly peruse them on their own. In Riesman's words, "The book, like the door, is an encouragement to isolation: the reader wants to be alone, away from the noise of others. . . . If oral communication keeps people together, print is the isolating medium *par excellence.*"[16] Silent reading—reading to oneself—became not only possible but the norm.

As more and more knowledge was created and accessed in isolation, people began to develop a new way of thinking about themselves: not as members of a community with no independent existence apart from the group but as separate, autonomous individuals. The significance of this change in perspective is illuminated by research performed in the early 1930s by a Soviet psychologist named Alexander Luria.[17] In informal interviews with illiterate peasants in remote regions of central Asia, Luria asked his subjects a number of questions about themselves. What sort of person are you? What's your character like? How would you describe yourself? What do you think of yourself? As members of a literate, highly self-conscious culture, we would find it easy to answer such questions, unless prevented by modesty from extolling our own virtues. But it was not modesty that caused the illiterate peasants to flounder when asked to engage in a process of self-assessment. Rather, as their responses reveal, they were simply unable to conceive of themselves as *selves*, with an independent existence apart from their social group. "How can I talk about my own character?" one of the interviewees replied. "Ask others; they can tell you about me. I myself can't say anything." Another responded on behalf of the group as a whole: "We behave well—if we were bad people, no one would respect us." Living in a pocket of the world little influenced by literacy, let alone typography, these peasants possessed a communal identity, gained not through solitary contemplation but through interaction with others.

Print, and the silent reading of printed texts, gave rise to the individual, the self writ large with a capital I. People began to regard their feelings and experiences as personal rather than shared phenomena, and letters and diaries—composed and read in solitude—became the popular means of expressing this newfound sense of self. Symptomatic of this newly emerged individuality was the appearance of the novel, which offered imaginative renderings of the new subjectivity. Written in the first person, early novels such as Daniel Defoe's *Robinson Crusoe* (1719) and Samuel Richardson's *Pamela* (1740) explored the changing nature of identity through the portrayal of "characters balanced (or torn) between individualism and communal identity"[18]—between the thought-worlds of literacy and orality.

Another conspicuous effect of the emergence of the individual was the concept of privacy, which, although foreign to oral societies, came to be perceived by people in typographic culture as a basic human need and right. "Reading and writing are private acts," writes Barry Sanders, "so private that they exert architectural force by demanding their own protected space"[19]—hence, house designs changed to accommodate the emergent need for private space. In short, people began to read quietly, to themselves and about themselves, in homes newly built to provide the requisite personal space.

Once again, these effects were not immediate. According to Eisenstein, it took a full century after the first book rolled off Gutenberg's press for a transformed European culture to emerge.[20] The psychological fallout—the profound changes in world view and habits of mind that I have outlined—would eventually follow. But in time, typography would shatter the enveloping sphere of acoustic space, creating a fragmented information environment in which the knower was separated from the known, knowledge was fractured into disciplines, and the individual was sundered from the tribe. And just as the alphabet had millennia before, the medium of print changed the way people thought. Introspection and independent thought became not only possible but, along with the analytic form of thought we call science, the new touchstones of truth and intelligence.

Moreover, these ways of knowing were increasingly described in terms appropriate to the newly exalted visual space in which they occurred. Knowing and understanding became synonymous with such ocular activities as perceiving or recognizing the truth, getting the picture, being enlightened or all-seeing, and having a point of view. Amidst this wealth of optical metaphors, it was perhaps only natural that one emergent habit of mind—the propensity to think deeply about ideas in conditions of quietude and solitude—would be designated in similar terms, as reflection.

* * *

This glimpse into the historical co-development of written language, typography, and the reflective intellect gives rise to new questions about the relationship between the acts of reading and writing and the development of reflective habits of mind. We need not subscribe to German biologist Ernst Haeckel's largely discredited Recapitulation Theory—the notion that an individual's maturation parallels our species' evolutionary development—in order to see echoes of the historical rise of the reflective mind, concomitant with the emergence of the alphabet and printed texts, whenever a young child learns to read and write.

Of course, it is possible to reflect without a pen or a book in hand. In fact, for years, I found my most richly reflective moments when taking Clancy, my canine companion, for an afternoon walk; others with whom I discuss reflection tell me that they find their opportunities for contemplation when running, painting, fly-fishing, or just lying in bed in the morning. But the association between literacy and reverie remains; the reflective person is often depicted as someone sitting with his nose in a book or with a pen in her hand poised over a pad of paper. In the next chapter, I therefore turn to the question: What is the nature of the connections between reading, writing, and reflection?

Chapter 4

READING, WRITING, AND REFLECTION

IN THE PREVIOUS CHAPTER I DESCRIBED THE RISE OF REFLECTION historically in terms of the impact of written and printed language on the social world and human consciousness. My interest in this chapter is exploring the nature of the relationships between reading, writing, and reflection at the level of the individual. In particular, I want to ask, are reading and writing prerequisites to reflection? And if so, what are the implications for education in the twenty-first century?

To begin, however, I will resume the historical survey of the last chapter and briefly trace the bell curve of literacy's rise and rumoured fall.

In the centuries following the development of the printing press, the written word became the chief means by which ideas circulated, and literacy was increasingly regarded as a fundamental characteristic of personhood, the unquestioned birthright of every member of European and North American society. Here is author Ursula K. Le Guin's tongue-in-cheek summary of the social change:

> In Europe, one can perceive through the Middle Ages a slow broadening of the light of the written word, which brightens into the Renaissance and shines out with Gutenberg. Then, before you know it, slaves are

reading, and revolutions are made with pieces of paper called Declarations of this and that, and schoolmarms replace gunslingers all across the Wild West, and people are mobbing the steamer delivering the latest installment of a new novel to New York, crying, "Is Little Nell dead? Is she dead?"[1]

Similarly, in his more sober portrait of small-town nineteenth-century America, Lionel Trilling conjures up a frontier world that "we would call primitive," but in which even the lowliest village labourers were reflective readers who participated freely in an ongoing discussion about literature and ideas. Trilling goes on to emphasize that, in nineteenth-century North America and Europe, literacy and literature "underlay every habit of mind." Professionals of all stripes—whether politicians or physicians— were expected to be well read, and "the man of original ideas spoke directly to 'the intelligent public.'"[2] That reading public, as indicated by an analysis of the readership of *The New-York Magazine; or, Literary Repository* in 1790, included the working masses, from shoemakers, grocers, and coppersmiths to bakers, barbers, and tavern keepers.[3] Jude Fawley, the book-obsessed stonemason in Thomas Hardy's *Jude the Obscure*, "read whenever he could as he walked to and from his work." But Jude was well aware that his propensity for reading and reflection did not set him apart from other labourers in nineteenth-century England—indeed, far from it, Jude realized that "by caring for books he was not escaping commonplace nor gaining rare ideas, every working-man being of that taste now."[4]

That, it would seem, is no longer the case. In 2007, the National Endowment for the Arts released a report with some rather alarming findings: in the United States, the amount of time spent reading declined sharply over the past 20 years to the point that the average American now spends about two hours of leisure time a day watching television and only seven minutes reading. Additionally, more and more Americans are considered non-readers; for example, from 1984 to 2004, the number of non-reading 17-year-olds more than doubled, from 9 percent to 19 percent. These findings have been corroborated by other reports, including a 2010 Scholastic study that found that both reading enjoyment and frequency among children tend to decline significantly with age. While most five- to eight-year-olds say they love reading or like it a lot and are moderate or high frequency readers, far fewer 15- to 17-year-olds enjoy reading and read for fun. The situation is not nearly so dire in Canada. However, a 2007 report issued by the Department of Canadian Heritage shows that Canadians on average spend 34 percent of their time watching television and surfing the Internet and only seven percent reading books. The growing issue, as all the reports make clear, is not so much illiteracy as aliteracy—people who can read, but choose not to.

Critic and essayist George Steiner refers to the emerging phenomenon of aliteracy as a "general 'retreat from the word,'"[5] and the nature of that retreat has been fully elaborated by French philosopher Jacques Ellul. In *The Humiliation of the Word*, Ellul argues that the primary cause of the growing devaluation of the word is the increasing precedence we give, as a society, to images, both still and moving, and what they communicate. For Ellul, the consequences of this devaluation of the written word are serious because the image promotes a superficial style of thought that differs radically from that to which the word gave rise. Therefore, as images increasingly dominate the classroom, along with the assumption that "an image teaches more in an instant than a long lecture,"[6] the implications for education, Ellul asserts, are rather grim: "thought is excluded by the continual invasion of images. . . . Such education is said to produce a critical mind and a capacity for judgment, whereas these are precisely what images eliminate . . . we are supposed to be freeing the human mind, but we are merely bogging it down more than ever in the exclusive visual world."[7] Here, Ellul is hinting at the possibility that a decline in literacy will go hand-in-hand with a decline in reflective thinking, a concern that Sven Birkerts makes explicit. Faced with the fact that "our age is leaving behind the habits of the book," Birkerts fears the irretrievable loss of "reverie and introspection" and "our access to the real complexity of the inner life."[8]

In the next chapter, I will further explore this possibility. *Is* reflection actually in decline? Here, however, I want to pursue those supposed connections between reading, writing, and reflection.

* * *

Many scholars and experts insist that there is indeed an intrinsic relationship between literacy and the impulse to reflect. This belief is shared by some of the students with whom I have spoken about reflection. "It's only reflective once the word gets down on paper," said one, while another told me, "I find myself getting really drawn into the written word. I find that a really compelling medium and it can cause me to reflect a lot." At the heart of this perceived association is the fact that, as one commentator asserts, "Both reading and writing consist of some degree of inwardness and withdrawal."[9] Both activities are best undertaken in conditions of solitude and silence, and even those who read on a noisy bus or write in a coffee shop must pull a curtain of quietude around themselves in order to create a space for reflection.

My recollections of my own experiences as a university student affirm what I hear from the students with whom I have spoken about reflection. In particular, as a doctoral student, I had the great privilege, as I now understand it, of being able to spend whole days reading and writing. Sometimes, I could be found sitting in front of my computer, painstakingly composing my thoughts; at other times, I could be found reading and scribbling notes in the margins of articles and books, or simply sitting in reverie. The relationships between reading, writing, and reflection evoked by this memory of my student experience are perhaps best described as reciprocal and circular: my in-depth reading of printed texts created a space for reflection, a process of synthesis during which new ideas emerged, which I then sought to articulate in writing. As I became intensely involved with my own written reflections, their reverberations imparted a new resonance to the printed texts with which I subsequently engaged, giving rise to new reflections, which I would again seek to capture in writing.

This circular model of the relationship between reading and writing elides the distinction between them: rather than being regarded as disconnected activities, they become phases in a single reflective process. As part of this process, reading is not a passive occupation but, as literacy expert Maryanne Wolf asserts, an active process, and one that becomes generative insofar as it prompts us "to go beyond the author's ideas to thoughts that are increasingly autonomous, transformative, and ultimately independent of the written text."[10] And writing—even just in the margins of the book, as we read—is the way we give form and substance to those intellectual resonances.

But the relationships between reading, writing, and reflection are more complex than this simple and rather idealized picture might suggest. Indeed, my memories of my doctoral student experiences go further, for I also recall that at some point in my studies I suddenly became aware of a phrase that popped up quite often in class discussions and conversations with my peers: they spoke about "writing up" their research. At first, the phrase simply puzzled me. As I have suggested, for me writing was (and continues to be) a highly reflective and generative process—and therefore a fundamental part of the research itself. When I sat down before the computer in the morning I never knew exactly where I would be by the end of the day: it was in the act of writing that I discovered where I was going. So what, I wondered, did my peers and professors mean when they spoke about "writing up" their research? Over time I began to understand that this phrase referred to a process of writing that seemed to me to be the furthest thing from the reflective act to which my days were devoted. "Writing up," as I finally found it described in books and other resources on conducting research, was highly structured and perfunctory. It appeared that, in writing up a dissertation, one did not engage so much with ideas as with data, using preapproved words and formats to present and discuss that data. What I was doing, on the other hand, might be called "writing down"—descending into a sea of ideas and taking the time to explore their dimensions and resonance.

If writing is not necessarily a reflective act, then, as Marcel Proust attests, the same can be said of reading. In his essay *On Reading*, Proust, a French novelist of the early twentieth century, explains that reading can serve as "the initiator, whose magic keys open to our innermost selves the doors of abodes into which we would not have known how to penetrate."[11] But this is not the case with all reading. The reflective intellect can be prodded into activity by a deep, slow, careful perusal during which the mind is hard at work synthesizing and speculating, personalizing information and integrating it into meaningful and perhaps entirely new patterns. Proust, however, argues that reading can actually stifle the reflective intellect when texts are simply regarded and read as if they are non-negotiable, providing not the basis for further thought but the final word on any subject:

> [R]eading becomes dangerous when . . . truth no longer appears to us as an ideal we can realize only through the intimate progress of our thought and the effort of our heart, but as a material thing, deposited between the leaves of books like honey ready-made for others.[12]

In this quote, Proust is describing precisely the way many students are taught to read textbooks and other assigned texts: in Dewey's words, "as ready-made intellectual pabulum to be accepted and swallowed just as if it were something bought at a shop."[13] This tendency is unfortunately perpetuated in adulthood. For example, the emergence of self-help books as the mainstay of bookstores in recent years suggests that adults, well-prepared by years of textbook reading, continue to seek unambiguous, unquestioned compendiums of information to be hastily mined for pertinent insights into various personal problems.

I suspect that, if asked whether reading always gives rise to reflection, most educators would, like Proust, answer in the negative and then proceed to exclude some texts on the basis of a tacit cultural standard. For surely the act of reading a Harlequin romance cannot be as generative of ideas, as *reflective*, as reading a Dickens novel, and surely writing an email message cannot be as reflective as composing an essay about one of Shakespeare's plays. This assumption—a source, perhaps, of reflection's elitist connotations—underlies many of the decisions that we make about the reading and writing activities of students, whether first graders or doctoral candidates. In fact, the notion that some texts are worth studying and some are not is the basis of most curricula.

While it may be true that some texts provide more meat for deep thought than others, the fact remains that many learners are quite able to read Shakespeare and other "great" works unreflectively. What Proust is suggesting is that the text itself matters less than the way the reader approaches it. No matter what the text, students' hasty, distracted scanning of required readings actually has the opposite of the desired effect, deadening the reflective intellect. As more and more reading, academic and otherwise, moves onscreen to e-books, e-readers, PDF files, and so forth, we must ask serious questions about whether the tendency toward hasty, superficial reading may be amplified in electronic environments. Both my experience and my research suggest that this is indeed the case, and I will have more to say about this in Chapter 6.

It is important to point out that the harmful effects of superficial reading are felt by teachers as well as students. More often than I care to admit I find myself scanning the abstracts of scholarly papers or flipping to the conclusion of an important book, and I know that I am not alone. In a 2007 study of academics at York University in Toronto, Heather Menzies and Janice Newson found that most of the university faculty they spoke with reported that they were not reading as deeply and reflectively as they used to. Instead, harried professors found themselves rushing through journal articles and other texts, "scanning, mining sources for selective bits of information" that they could drop into their own work.[14]

Language arts specialist James Moffett makes a case similar to Proust's for excluding some writing activities from the reflective circle, not on the basis of what is written, but why. Moffett's argument hinges upon his distinction between writing as "copying and transcribing, paraphrasing and plagiarizing" and "authentic *authoring*."[15] He contends that only when students write to give form to their own inchoate contemplations do they enter the symbiotic circle, "the give-and-take of minds and voices [that] can lift each member beyond where he or she started. . . . If practiced as real authoring, not disguised playback, writing *discovers* as much as it communicates."[16] A doctoral student with whom I spoke echoed this understanding of writing as authoring—as a reflective process of making connections and finding meaning:

> When you're reflecting in writing you're also constructing your own voice and putting onto paper your own thoughts, so you can shape it, delete it, add to it, or whatever—and you come up with something. That's the writing piece, just the reflecting itself. . . . It's that set time to stop and think.

To summarize, I have suggested that there are connections between reading, writing, and reflection. Individuals who read widely and willingly, and who are inclined to articulate their ideas in writing, generally have more opportunity to engage in reflective thought than those who read and write little or not at all. Reading and writing can be intensely reflective acts when practiced mindfully and meaningfully. However, it is also the case that reading and writing can actually derail reflection if undertaken for trivial reasons or in a superficial, perfunctory way.

This conclusion, of course, has some rather startling implications for pedagogy. By way of exploring those implications let me turn for a moment to another student experience from my past, this one from my undergraduate years. Specifically, I will hark back, with some mortification, to an assignment I wrote many years ago: ten laboriously crafted pages on images of light and dark in *Romeo and Juliet*. If we proceed with the assumption that engaging with high-flown texts somehow gives rise to high-flown thoughts, then we would regard my reading of the play and subsequent composition of a paper about it as an excellent opportunity for reflection. In fact, nothing could be further from the truth. I read the play because it was an assigned text in a survey course on Shakespeare; the superficiality of my chosen topic indicates how little thought I gave, or wanted to give, to it. My reading entailed scanning the text for metaphors of light ("It is the east, and Juliet is the sun. / Arise, fair sun, and kill the envious moon"[17]), and most of my writing time was devoted not to thought about the topic but to leafing through the thesaurus, searching for impressive polysyllabic words that would lend weight to writing that was otherwise light as a feather. And yet, as I recall, this paltry effort somehow merited an "A"—which, in the end, was all that I sought.

My point is that it is unlikely that reading assigned texts and writing assigned papers will activate the reflective intellect, nor will any kind of reading or writing activity in which the purpose, content, or form are given to learners—and what is more, given en masse—rather than drawn from the individual learner's own need to articulate meaning.

The important implication for me, as a teacher, is that I cannot mandate reflection. Simply asking learners to reflect—for example, by keeping reflective journals, a common practice in teacher education programs—is unlikely to ignite the reflective intellect.[18] That is precisely what another graduate student told me:

> The only way for you to, I imagine, get a chance to share in my reflection is if I write it down. So there are constant assignment protocols that I've experienced, where a reflective journal, or an assignment that involves reflecting upon an author's words in an article, is put into place through a written assignment. . . . [But] I just wonder if reflection is more beneficial for me if I don't have to make you understand my thinking at any one point in time. So if I'm writing it down, I'm always conscious of the way you will interpret my words and so I have to take real care in the way I've presented it to you. Which goes beyond the thought processes that I have if I was reflecting on something.

I am caught, then, within a conundrum: because the workings of the reflective mind are invisible, I require material evidence that my students are indeed reflecting. However, the minute I reduce reflection to assigned writing or reading, something learners are expected to do, for which they will receive a mark, the authenticity of the reflective experience is compromised, and reflection itself is trivialized.

It becomes clear that although reflection exists within a web of words, not all words will do, and some might actually have the effect of derailing reflective thought. Specifically, the reflective intellect is likely to be engaged by reading that is undertaken as a means of personal interest or fulfillment, not in order to acquire, temporarily, the knowledge needed to pass an examination. Reflective writing should be a spontaneous articulation of the workings of the mind rather than a staged response to an assignment—even if the assignment is simply to express one's thoughts.

All this suggests what may seem, for educators, a discouraging conclusion: reflection is not a skill that can be taught. However, as a habit of mind and a way of being, it can be fostered, and in the final chapter I will elaborate upon what this means, both within the context of the school and the constraints of schooling.

Chapter 5

IS REFLECTION IN DECLINE?

WE HAVE SEEN THAT WITH THE ADVENT OF WRITTEN LANGUAGE and typography a new habit of mind was nourished and cultivated: reflection. However, with the rise, in the nineteenth and twentieth centuries, of a Western culture that gave precedence to scientific truth and technological efficiency, contemplative thought fell out of favour and became conceptually divorced from real life and its practicalities. In co-opting reflection to describe scientific process and practical action, Dewey, Schön, and their followers were implicitly privileging the technical mindset while devaluing less rational forms of mental activity, which were dismissed as random, purposeless, and chaotic. With reflection (as they redefined it) available to everyone, even those who never had the opportunity to stop and think, reflection in its conventional sense (related to solitude and slowness) fell further out of favour. As a result, more and more value was placed upon a capability for instrumental action and rapid reaction. And as we become increasingly unwilling and unable to stop and think, reflection continues its long decline.

Or does it? Some commentators insist that, to the contrary, the flourishing products of human ingenuity and innovation that surround us are concrete evidence of vast improvements in human cognition. But of course, the ability to create such technologies is one thing; the proclivity to contemplate the proper ends of innovation is quite another. In books such as *The*

Technological Society and *The Technological System*, Jacques Ellul describes in detail how the expansion of the technological system—the integrated, self-regulated network of televisions, computers, telephones, BlackBerrys, iPods, and other devices—has become an end in itself that flourishes at the expense of humane concepts, but only insofar as we increasingly fail to stop and think about how the proliferation of technology affects the quality of human life.

Ellul is but one of many astute observers of the state of contemporary society who insist that the reflective intellect is in retreat. Alberto Manguel concurs that "depth of reflection, slowness of advancement, difficulty of undertakings" are "almost lost qualities."[1] We live in a time, he laments, when "answers are offered instead of questions, and instant and superficial gratification takes the place of difficulty and depth."[2] Similarly, David Geoffrey Smith observes that Western civilization is currently witnessing "the gradual evacuation of the inner life of people, and the production of a form of humanity concerned only with surfaces."[3] And Martin Heidegger claims that "man today is in flight from thinking":

> Let us not fool ourselves. All of us, including those who think professionally, as it were, are often enough thought-poor; we are all far too easily thought-less. Thoughtlessness is an uncanny visitor who comes and goes everywhere in today's world. For nowadays we take in everything in the quickest and cheapest way, only to forget it just as quickly, instantly.[4]

Heidegger is well aware that most people "will flatly deny this flight from thinking" and, citing the flourishing of research and invention, "will assert the opposite."[5] But the products of science and technology, Heidegger explains, arise from what he calls "calculative thinking," what I referred to in an earlier chapter as rational thought. This kind of thinking "never stops, never collects itself. Calculative thinking is not meditative thinking, not thinking which contemplates the meaning which reigns in everything that is."[6]

* * *

While Heidegger and other social critics are dismissive of assertions that the human mind is evolving to a new level, they rarely offer positive evidence in support of their own claims of reflection's demise. Of course, there can be no formal, objective studies to support, or disprove, the assertion that reflection is in decline. Apart from the difficulties inherent in conducting such a study, the attempt to do so—to submit reflective thought to the dictates of calculation—would be, in itself, evidence of a severe social devaluation of reflection. But does that mean that the decline of reflection is visible only to the reflective mind?

In fact, it often seems to me that I am surrounded by clear signs of the decline of reflection, many of them, as might be expected, in the realm of human communications, where an increasing trend toward banality seems to clearly signal the dwindling depth of thought. Consider the increasing superficiality of television news coverage. In the 1950s, Edward R. Murrow and other journalists regarded television as a means of continuing the serious dialogue about important issues that was already taking place on the radio. When I turn on today's news, however, what I find is that "thought" pieces have devolved into Andy Rooneyish rants and reasoned social discourse into *Piers Morgan Tonight*, while serious news content is usurped by celebrities' hijinks. The result is that information we receive about our world tends increasingly toward the trivial and the inane.

Consider also the dumbing down of political discourse. My touchstone in this area is the Lincoln-Douglas debates that took place in the American Midwest in 1858. From August to October of that year, Abraham Lincoln, then a relative new-comer to the political scene, engaged Senator Stephen Douglas in a series of debates in seven locations throughout Illinois. Each debate lasted at least three hours, some as long as seven, allowing for lengthy statements and rebuttals by both candidates. Despite the length of the debates and the scorching sun overhead, the audiences were huge (the first two debates were attended by 12,000 and 15,000 people, respectively) and "wildly responsive."[7] The attentiveness and interest of those present is evident in the debate transcripts, which are peppered with commentary and questions, cheers and boos, from the audience. Today, in contrast, we display a diminished willing-ness and ability to attend to reflective individuals giving voice to their thoughts. We want our politicians to communicate in dynamic snippets. "Dead air," the pregnant pause during which a political candidate formulates an intelligent response, becomes an invitation to channel surf.

Then there is the impoverished nature of the business com-munications that circulate in offices everywhere. Letter-writing was once virtually synonymous with reflection. Correspondents would commonly spend hours, sometimes days, crafting their epistles, and because the process of writing a letter entailed solitude, silence, and slowness, much of the content was inevi-tably reflective. Today, the art of letter-writing is in a rapid freefall, as people dash off email messages and Twitter posts (or "tweets") that are likely to be read with as little care as they were written. Those letters that are composed for business purposes tend to be highly formulaic, made up almost entirely of trite, stilted, and unnecessarily long-winded phrases ("at the present time," "we are of the opinion that," "make a concerted effort") that can be combined like building blocks—or, as George Orwell puts it in his brilliant essay on "Politics and the English Language," "tacked together like the sections of a prefabricated hen-house."[8] This over-reliance on formulaic, wordy expressions and vague, vogue words is compensatory, imparting to professional communications a weightiness that was once derived from the substance of the ideas expressed. According to essayist John Ralston Saul, "These mythological words come to replace thought. They are the modern equivalent of an intellectual void."[9]

Letter-writing is not the only aspect of professional communications that can be brought forward as evidence of reflection's decline. The business world has also given rise to the custom of enhancing oral presentations to colleagues or clients with slideware programs, such as PowerPoint. In *The Cognitive Style of PowerPoint*, Edward Tufte, an expert on the visual presentation of information, describes the use of slideware as "contrary to serious thinking."[10] Because ideas are generally too complex and ambiguous for representation in the reductive formats of a PowerPoint slide, most slideware-assisted presentations are restricted to the realm of factual information. Certainly, a presenter may start out wishing to communicate serious ideas, but because the medium predisposes users to conceptualize their topics from the beginning in terms of cryptic, decontextualized bulleted points, the products of deep thought will inevitably be diminished, lost, or transmuted into information along the way. And any ideas that somehow manage to survive being "PowerPointed" will likely be obscured by the dynamic imagery and technical virtuosity of the visual display. Having watched with dismay as the stimulating intellectual sharing at the heart of the academic conference has given way, during the past decade, to a deadly enumeration of bulleted points, I am both bewildered and aghast at the rapid inroads that PowerPoint is making into elementary, secondary, and post-secondary classrooms.

* * *

And what about the classroom? Reflection would appear to be in dramatic retreat in the sphere of human communications—increasingly, we are hurling sound bytes, PowerPointing ideas to death, and pressing the send button without stopping to think—but is that same decline evident in the kinds of transactions that tend to take place in schools?

The short answer is yes. Given the pressures to teach everything that must be taught and subsequently tested in a school year, teachers rarely have time to stop and think. This theme is expressed in the two quotations below. The first is from a teacher, and the second is from a former teacher who worked for many years as a school administrator:

> Very seldom do teachers have time to think about what they accomplished through the day, what they're planning to do as a result of that, or how they relate what they do to what their peers do. . . . Teachers just don't generally have much time . . . it's an uncommon thing for me for teachers to have a reflective practice in their work.

> I have a huge respect for teachers and I think the majority of teachers do yeoman service; they're going 90 miles an hour. When I have teacher conversations with former colleagues and those that are right in the trenches now, they're

so busy with the day-to-day operations of the classroom, I
don't think they would say, you know, I'm thinking about
this or I'm thinking about that or I'm reflecting on this.

Of course, the work of a teacher has always entailed more
than delivering instruction, but even more so today, when teachers are also expected to serve as counselors, behavioural manag-
ers, technicians, mentors, and job coaches, to name just a few
roles. Yet at the same time, fundamental trust in the ability of
teachers to do their jobs is eroding, replaced by an over-reliance
on standardized tests that serve to ensure teacher "accountability" while contributing even more to teachers' workloads.

Amidst the tumult of a typical teaching day, reflection falls by
the wayside. Speaking from personal experience, elementary school
teacher Ronna Scott Mosher eloquently sums up the situation:

> There are many times in teaching when it seems that we
> live in the midst of a din we ourselves have created and
> can no longer hear, a constant noise that may interfere
> with our hearing what it is we talk about, what it is that
> we wish to understand.[11]

Teachers, of course, are not alone in having to contend with a
host of responsibilities during the course of a single workday,
but one of their important roles is to serve as exemplars, to
model ways of being in the world. Children learn something
when they see their role model rushing around, filling fleeting moments during the day with day-plans, report cards, and
other busywork. They learn something quite different when
they see their teacher sitting quietly with a book, relishing an
opportunity for silence and reverie.

What, then, of students? Since few if any of the carefully apportioned segments of school time are devoted to reflection, the reality is that today's children have little opportunity, and therefore little inclination, to just sit and think. The result is what teacher-educator David Geoffrey Smith describes as "the depth of depthlessness in the contemporary classroom":[12]

> The rapid flitting from one topic to another, one country after another, one activity followed by another activity, not only reflects the hyperkinetic quality of contemporary life in the technical, industrialized world, but also the lifeworld of the learning atmosphere oriented toward a profound superficiality, to say which is not oxymoronic. . . . Pedagogy is reduced to a pointing to the parade of facts and information available through the multiple technologies of the age.[13]

The incessant busyness continues outside the classroom walls as children are shuttled from school to afterschool programs, hockey games, ballet, and piano lessons. Such extracurricular activities promote their development as well-rounded, confident individuals, but—along with television and computer time—they usurp the quiet, self-sustaining moments of reading and reverie that are necessary to promote children's growth in other areas: in particular, to nourish the development of a reflective intellect.

Also impinging upon the place of reflection in educational institutions is the growing popularity of social constructivist pedagogies. Briefly, constructivist epistemology states that knowledge is not delivered by a teacher or teaching machine to a passive learner but is constructed by the individual based upon his or her experiences. Social constructivism, based largely on the work of Russian psychologist Lev Vygotsky, posits that a child's cognitive abilities and structures develop through interactions with others. As social constructivism flourishes within educational discourses and practices, group work becomes foundational at all levels, leaving less time for individuals to construct knowledge and understanding during moments of independent, silent reverie. In fact, the image of children working alone—seated, heads down, in rigid rows of desks—has become a clichéd emblem for the lock-step, supposedly mind-deadening pedagogy that prevailed decades ago, before we came to our senses and adopted constructivist practices. It is worth considering the possibility that, in rejecting that model, we have allowed the pendulum to swing too far in the opposite direction.

* * *

I have established that the reality of contemporary life provides both adults and children with few opportunities and incentives for reflection, and many barriers that not only inhibit the inclination to stop and think but cause us to devalue it as a way of thinking and being in the world. But is reflection's decline simply a matter of reduced opportunity and a concomitant devaluation of reverie, or is something else at play? Are all of us, young and not so young, increasingly less apt to stop and think because we choose not to, or because we no longer possess the intellectual ability to do so?

This would seem to be a vital question, especially for educators. After all, if learners are not engaging in reflective thought because they do not value silent introspection, that is one thing; if they are not reflecting because they simply are unable to do so, that is quite another.

Or is it? I believe that reflection's decline is a matter of social changes that have resulted in the devaluation of slow, careful thought. This devaluation places us in an extremely precarious position because the intellectual capabilities we choose not to use today may very well become unavailable to us tomorrow.

There is a precedent for this belief, for that is, in fact, precisely what happened in the case of another intellectual faculty: memory. In the fourth century BC, Socrates sounded a stern note of warning about memory's decline that went largely unheeded. Until that time, Greek culture had been preserved from generation to generation within the human memory, a vast repository that contained everything that was known—in effect, a living library. Watching the written word make inroads into his oral culture, Socrates lamented that the ability to write things down would "implant forgetfulness" in his students, becoming a memory crutch.[14]

Of course, history has proven Socrates correct. Ultimately, what written language changed was the *value* placed upon memory. Once it was possible to record in writing all of a society's wisdom and lore, the respect that had hitherto been accorded to those who remembered—the elders, the storytellers, the teachers—became severely diminished. At first, if people did not bother remembering, it was because they chose not to. But today, after generations of opting not to exert our memories, choice is no longer an issue. The capacious memory palaces that once soared in each human mind have crumbled, to be replaced by Post-it Notes and handheld electronic planners.

In the same way, the contemporary devaluation of reflection may presage its genuine decline. Increasingly, our day-to-day activities entail navigating a high-speed, perpetually changing, interactive, hyperactive, electric media-sphere in which the value accorded to reflection—the inclination to stop and think—is rapidly diminishing. And that which we now devalue may become, through disuse, lost to us forever, as educational psychologist Jane Healy cautions:

> The human brain has survived and flourished because its plasticity enables it to adapt in wondrous ways to changing environments. Electronic worlds will inevitably influence its functioning, whether for better or worse depends on decisions we make now. Mental habits, once formed, stick with the individual and also with the general society. Likewise, skills such as literacy or the ability to reflect deeply, if lost to a generation, may not be regained.[15]

My instinct at this point is to back up Healy's dire warning with descriptions of studies in neuroscience and psychology which confirm not only that repeated exposure to television, cell phones, podcasts, email, and other information streams shapes the child's "plastic," growing brain, but that, when grey matter increases in those parts of the brain that support multitasking and visual-spatial intelligence, it correspondingly decreases in other parts supporting reflection and abstract thought. However, given that I have been highly critical of the tendency to privilege scientific, verifiable evidence over the insights of the reflective mind, I will resist that impulse. Instead, I will invoke the words of philosopher William Barrett, who shrewdly encapsulates the implications of such research in his bleak warning that, if we allow our capacity for reflection to simply slip away, "[w]e may become no longer free for the kind of thinking that would redeem us from the world we ourselves have created."[16]

Healy and Barrett echo some of the themes and concerns I have heard voiced in my discussions with students, teachers, parents, and others—discussions that suggest the difficulty of sustaining reflective habits of mind amidst the flourishing of technological innovation and, inextricably related to emergent media, an accelerating pace of life. It seems that, in trying to keep pace with our digital devices (whose processing speed is doubling every two years or so), we also become information processors, judging ourselves and others by the same criteria— speed, efficiency, accuracy—that one would use to judge the merits of a machine. Increasingly, slow, silent thought falls by the wayside. Far from being a quality that will help us get ahead in this fast-paced world, a reflective habit of mind may actually be considered a liability, interfering with all the things that must be done in the course of a busy workday. Increasingly, the people we admire, and those who achieve success in a world revved up to machine pace, are not reflective but *reactive*, capable of responding to situations as spontaneously as video game players react to the vivid, over-stimulating prompts and signals on the screen.

Contemporary technology thus arises as a significant obstacle to reflection because of the manic pace it sets, a pace that makes it untenable and undesirable for its human operators to simply stop and think. And information technology further works against reflection by offering us an endless array of fascinating distractions that gobble up what little free time we might have, as well as time that might otherwise have been spent more productively. My students tell me that they spend hours of every day compulsively playing video games, texting messages with their cell phones, loitering on Facebook—hyperactivities that preclude the possibility of reflection. And, if I am completely honest, I will admit that I too spend more and more unnecessary hours in front of the computer screen, hours I might otherwise have used to just stop and think.

As a teacher, I want to help my students rediscover the value of reflection, but how can I begin to compete with the irresistible lure of the screen? Is the answer, as so many educators insist, to bring computers into the classroom? I believe not, for as technology moves into classrooms in which teachers and learners are already driven by the unrelenting demands of curriculum coverage, the pace is merely ratcheted up another notch. Some time ago, for example, I listened with dismay to a radio interview in which a teacher enthused that, now that her students all had laptops, they were able to complete a unit on Edgar Allan Poe in one day rather than two weeks. Many other educators insist that the answer is to insert ourselves behind that endlessly fascinating screen, but how can online instruction hold a candle to the temptations of Twitter, "CrackBerry," and other technologies that feed what seems to be a communication addiction?

These musings give rise to a very important and disquieting question: Is reflection irreconcilable with the encroaching presence of information technology?

Chapter 6

REFLECTION AND TECHNOLOGY

I HAVE BEFORE ME A COLLECTION OF RECENT BOOKS AND articles with provocative titles such as *iBrain: Surviving the Technological Alteration of the Modern Mind*, "Dumbed Down: The Troubling Science of How Technology is Rewiring Kids' Brains," *The Dumbest Generation: How the Digital Age Stupefies Young Americans and Jeopardizes Our Future*, *The Shallows: What the Internet is Doing to Our Brains*, and "Is Google Making Us Stupid?"[1]

Clearly, the shared concern underlying all of these pieces is that when we use technology—computers and the Internet, but also cell phones, iPods, BlackBerrys, and other devices that compel and distract—our minds are somehow being rewired in ways that short-circuit the reflective intellect. Here is how Nicholas Carr described what is happening in a controversial 2008 *Atlantic* article that produced a plethora of heated online commentary:

> Over the past few years I've had an uncomfortable sense that someone, or something, has been tinkering with my brain, remapping the neural circuitry, reprogramming the memory. My mind isn't going—so far as I can tell—but it's changing. I'm not thinking the way I used to think. . . . I think I know what's going on. For more than a decade now, I've been spending a lot of time online, searching

and surfing, and sometimes adding to the great databases
of the Internet. . . . And what the Net seems to be doing is
chipping away my capacity for concentration and contemplation. My mind now expects to take in information the
way the Net distributes it: in a swiftly moving stream of
particles. Once I was a scuba diver in a sea of words. Now
I zip along the surface like a guy on a Jet Ski.[2]

It is instructive to contrast Carr's observations with those
made in another *Atlantic* article, some 63 years earlier. In "As
We May Think," Vannevar Bush, then Director of the U.S.
Office of Scientific Research and Development, optimistically
proposed a system of knowledge storage and retrieval that he
called the "memex."[3] A memex, Bush wrote, "is a device in
which an individual stores all his books, records, and communications, and which is mechanized so that it may be consulted
with exceeding speed and flexibility. It is an enlarged intimate
supplement to his memory."[4] As a hypothetical means of accessing information and following associative trails at the click of a
button, Bush's memex is generally considered to be the concep-
tual forerunner of the web's hypertext. The important point is
that Bush regarded the memex as a means of mechanically supporting human memory in the face of the "growing mountain"
of information that was confronting people even as long ago
as 1945.[5] This, he hoped, would free minds for what he called
"mature" or creative thought—in other words, reflection—for
which there are no mechanical aids.[6] The ultimate purpose of
the memex was to increase our store of wisdom and to elevate
the human spirit, and the quality of life, accordingly.

In the early days of computing, Bush's optimistic sense of
the potential of the machine to liberate the greater powers of the

human mind held sway. Although some commentators urged that we stop and think about the experiment we were conducting with our minds and our children's minds, unquestioning enthusiasm for digital devices and their pedagogical possibilities continued to snowball during the 1960s, 70s, 80s, and 90s. Indeed, it was generally assumed that merely interacting with a computer somehow conferred intelligence upon the user. Despite its physical similarity to the television screen, which was commonly disparaged as "the boob tube" and "the idiot box," most people seemed to feel that interactions with the computer screen were a form of intellectual self-improvement—an assumption that hardware and software corporations did their best to promote in advertisements. As recently as 1997, Paul Levinson insisted that "a computer screen is not a television" because

> in contrast [to television viewers], users of computer screens are interacting with the computer—they are participants in what is happening on the screen, since they are often its very creators—rather than passive observers. They sit up, faces alert, a few inches from the screen, and constantly control what they see via keyboard or mouse, in sharp distinction to "couch potatoes" who only trouble to change the channel by remote control during commercials or between programs.[7]

Given this commonly accepted distinction between the two screens, the parent who experienced pangs of guilt when little Johnny or Susie sat for hours with eyes glued to the screen of the "electric babysitter" could actually be pleased and proud to see Johnny or Susie sitting in a similar posture of engrossed contemplation before the computer screen. The former image connoted mindless passivity, while the latter image was often featured on the covers of books about computer-based instruction, where it was meant to serve as an emblem of the kind of keen intellectual involvement with which one receives the material displayed upon the computer screen.

However, to judge from the spate of recent books and articles on how technology is eroding our intellectual capacity, the assumption that people, and particularly young people, who spend hours in front of the computer are improving their minds (an assumption that fuelled the push to computerize classrooms) is in the process of being resoundingly overturned. Now, according to a *Maclean's* article on "How Computers Make Our Kids Stupid," we are confronting mounting evidence "that our obsessive use of information technology is dumbing us down, adults as well as kids."[8] For example, a 2005 study commissioned by Hewlett Packard found that the IQ of office workers trying to cope with the onslaught of email messages while also doing their work fell by 10 points. This loss of intellectual capacity is, as those reporting the research provocatively pointed out, the equivalent to missing a whole night's sleep and more than twice the four-point drop in IQ associated with smoking marijuana.[9]

Given his high hopes for the memex, Bush would likely be appalled to see how things have actually turned out. Rather than enhancing our capabilities and opportunities for reflection, information technology seems to have become one of the greatest obstacles to deep thought.

What happened?

* * *

A primary theme of this book is that the introduction of a new communications technology, from the alphabet to the Internet, has consequences (often unanticipated) for social arrangements and interactions, and ultimately for habits of mind. These changes are not instantaneous; it takes some time for the implications of a new medium of communication within a particular context to work themselves out and become apparent. While Vannevar Bush is often acclaimed for his foresight in envisaging the Internet, what he failed to anticipate was that, over time, as the online computer became an increasingly inescapable part of social life and intellectual processes, we would lose our bearings in the very mountains of information that he hoped his memex would make more manageable.

Few commentators have written more cogently about the rise of information and what it means for humanity than Neil Postman. In *Technopoly*, Postman describes how the telegraph first created the concept of information—facts and bits of knowledge that could be ripped from their context and sent down an electric wire to distant places, where they became commodities, "bought and sold irrespective of [their] uses or meaning."[10] In England, one of the first feats of the telegraph was to spread the word about the birth of Queen Victoria's second son, Alfred, in 1844. Thanks to the new technology, the *Times* of London was out with the news within 40 minutes, "declaring itself 'indebted to the extraordinary power of the Electro-Magnetic Telegraph' for providing the information so quickly."[11] Of course, the lives of British citizens were not tangibly improved by this knowledge, but the ability to quickly receive such fragments of disconnected, fundamentally meaningless information somehow created an appetite for more. And as new technologies such as radio and television added to the volume of information, and sped up the means by which it could be collected, distributed, and accessed, the pace of life increased accordingly. People were expected to receive and process information as quickly as it was sent.

That expectation becomes problematic in the age of the Internet. Today, the average person encounters more information in the run of a day than a contemporary of Shakespeare would likely have been exposed to in his or her entire lifetime. Much of this information resides online, in the free-for-all of web pages, widgets and apps, video and audio: a constant stream coming at us from desktop, laptop, and handheld devices. For computer users, and particularly young computer users, being online increasingly entails moving fluidly among several information streams at the same time. And as computer processing power doubles approximately every two years, we are confronted with an ever-growing torrent of information surging forth at an ever-faster pace: the analogy often used is that of drinking out of a fire hose. Information coming at us in exponentially increasing quantities and speeds becomes, as Postman observes, "a form of garbage, not only incapable of answering the most fundamental human questions but barely useful in providing coherent direction to the solution of even mundane problems."[12]

Vannevar Bush's memex was intended to help people make time for reflection by providing a way to manage the information overload that was already looming in the mid-1940s. What Bush could not anticipate, however, was that, in the race to keep up with the increasing volume and speed of information, slow, careful thought—the kind of thought that is needed to understand the human consequences of technological innovation—would be pushed to the sidelines. Nor could he have foreseen that, at some point, the mundane thrill of surfing the information ocean, confronting the continually breaking waves, would become a compulsion, giving rise to a profoundly heightened attention to the multitudinous fragments of information that surround us.

This emergent, rapidly shifting, perpetually overstimulated form of awareness has been called "hyper attention"[13] and "continuous partial attention."[14] Both terms describe a state of mind that is characterized by "switching focus rapidly among different tasks, preferring multiple information streams, seeking a high level of stimulation, and having a low tolerance for boredom."[15] Another term that is often used to describe the phenomenon is "media multitasking," but this is a misnomer. While multitasking was an early byproduct of the information society's demand that we keep pace with our machines by becoming efficient processors of information, continuous partial attention emerges as a way of living and knowing in a network society. Increasingly, identity and social status are determined in the same way as the Google search engine ranks web pages—according to the number of other nodes in the network to which one is connected. The upshot is that hyper-attentive individuals live in a state of heightened vigilance, perpetually on the alert for a new message, a new contact, a new fragment of information—even if it is an instant messaging conversation about nothing or a cell phone call that serves no real purpose. Solitude, in the world of hyper attention, is not only undesirable but to be feared: to be unconnected, to be unseen and alone, is simply to not exist.

Continuous partial attention manifests itself when individuals who are engaged in a computer-based task (such as inputting data, using a word processor to write a report, or participating in an online course) find themselves at the same time continuously scanning and monitoring the periphery, and immediately shifting their focus when they receive email alerts, instant messages, or calls on their cell phones. To gain a better understanding of what continuous partial attention really means, and how this constant state of distraction and hypervigilance works against reflection, consider what one of my students wrote at the beginning of an assignment in order to dramatically represent the pull of technology in his life:

> Okay, I have one more assignment to do this semester. Then I can go back to whatever it is I am doing. . . . Okay, first thing's first. I must open a blank Microsoft Word document. Hmmm . . . well first I'll just open up an Internet Explorer window and check my email and Facebook. No new messages. I'll just check up on the Blue Jays' off-season activity too. . . . Well, I guess there are no new Google News items on the subject since I last checked two hours ago. While I'm at it though, I might as well open two more tabs and see how the Toronto Raptors and the Boston Bruins did in their games last night. . . . What are you doing? . . . I think you need to go to the library and sit down in a cubicle with a pen and some paper. That's a good idea. Your computer is turning every passing thought into a time-consuming online endeavor. You need to unplug yourself in order to make any serious progress.

Although this was written by a young man, it is becoming increasing clear that, in the Internet age, people of all ages who sit in front of a computer do so in a state of hyper attention. As I write this, for example, my email lurks in the background, and although I have deliberately disabled the audio email alert, I am all too frequently tempted to check if any new messages have arrived. Like video game players, we are constantly on the alert, our eyes darting, our fingers twitching, anxious not to let one message, one fragment of information, one potential contact with a virtual friend slip by. And somehow, amidst the riot of online communications and connections, we become disconnected from that part of ourselves that is inclined to stop and consider other ways of being in the world.

Those who sing the praises of the network society emphasize the value of connectivity. The metaphor of the network naturally amplifies the importance of the interconnection of nodes, consisting of both people and information nuggets, in our information-saturated society. But the hyper-connection of millions of nodes, many both fleeting and trivial, has nothing to do with reflection, and in fact actually works against reflective habits of mind by giving rise to a superabundance of information that defies integration, and to a self that is terrified by the silence and solitude of disconnection.

* * *

We are only beginning to explore what the emergent cognitive style of short and constantly shifting attention means for teaching and learning. Yet the consequences are bound to be significant because teaching as we know it is essentially the business of capturing and holding attention. It is based upon the premise that learners will be able to perform one task at a time without distraction before moving on to another, which is why many learning difficulties are attributed to short attention spans or attention deficiencies.

Most approaches to technology-based instruction are similarly based upon the premise that focused attention is a prerequisite for learning. In fact, one of the primary rationales for using technology and multimedia in the delivery of instruction is to increase learner engagement with the instructional content. The generally accepted but untested premise is that children using educational programs that incorporate games and glitz will learn while having fun. More recently, technologies such as PowerPoint and YouTube have become standard fare in the classroom in an attempt to make drab lessons more appealing to a generation raised on television and video games.

The problem with such attempts to use technology to engage learners who are accustomed to paying continuous partial attention is that the educational use of multimedia may actually exacerbate the situation. As teachers strive to compete with the multitude of distractions, they must continually up the ante: lessons become more dynamic and computer-based instructional materials grow flashier, louder, and glitzier, more akin to video games. Such practices, however, simply perpetuate a culture of hyper-stimulation and are, as a result, deeply inimical to reflection.

The pedagogical implications of hyper attention expand when we consider that more and more of the reading students do for their courses and research takes place on a computer that is also the "gateway" to a host of distracting activities, from emailing, gaming, and instant messaging to social networking and web surfing.[16] Walter Ong observes that "Print . . . situates utterance and thought on a surface disengaged from everything else,"[17] but that is profoundly untrue of the text that appears online, whether in the form of e-books, web pages, or PDF files. In a recent study inquiring into university students' experiences of reading onscreen, I found that, while students are developing strategies to help minimize distraction in the space around them (for example, by blocking out ambient noise with music, the "new silence"[18]), they are generally less able to ignore the fascinating distractions that reside on the screen itself.[19] Here is how a couple of students explained it:

> The computer is right there; if I have MSN on and somebody goes dadoop, there's a message, sometimes I'll try to ignore it to get to the end of the paragraph, but oftentimes even though I'm reading I'm still thinking in my head, I wonder what they want?

> I'm wasting more time not reading than reading, you know, with email and talking to other people. If it was a book I would read more than if it was online because there are more distractions, easier ways to, oh, I'm just going to check this, and totally forget that you're reading, and then an hour or two goes by and you're like, I guess I should go back.

Thus, as we might expect, continuous partial attention derails the slow, solitary, and therefore essentially reflective experience of reading.

The same issues of attention and distraction apply within the "wired" classroom. Far from enhancing pedagogy, these expensive high-tech learning environments give rise to a host of new problems, particularly the increasing prevalence of students who spend class time instant messaging, watching movies, or just surfing the Internet. Any educator hoping to create an atmosphere conducive to slow, deep thought is inevitably defeated by such "progressive" measures.

However, the effects of continuous partial attention are perhaps most keenly felt when instruction moves entirely to online environments. Recently, compelled to inquire into the implications of this fractured focus for the online teaching and learning that is becoming increasingly prevalent in post-secondary education, I conducted a qualitative inquiry with university students taking e-learning courses.[20] My goal was to gain insight into their experiences of attention and distraction, and I was not surprised to learn that students feel that they cope with more distractions when participating in online courses than when in the classroom. Unexpectedly, however, I also found that students are in the process of reconceptualizing "distraction": study participants regard cell phone calls and email alerts less as impediments to learning that break concentration than as necessary interruptions for individuals unaccustomed to long periods of focus. As one student said, "I find the multitasking ability that online learning allows you to do keeps me working for longer." "Focus" itself is being redefined in similar terms. While many of the students I surveyed and interviewed indicated they were focused more intently in online courses than when sitting in a classroom, they added that focus for them took place in "spurts of 20 minutes or so," during which they might check their email two or three times. As post-secondary institutions respond to student demands, as well as the necessity of expanding their customer base, by putting more and more courses online, it behooves us to ask where, amidst the flash and lure of online diversions, our students will carve out a space for reflection.

In "Burnt Norton," written in 1935, poet T.S. Eliot prophetically describes this new state of mind as being "distracted from distraction by distraction." Like so many people today, the students I studied demonstrate a restless urge to troll for messages in online spaces, an urge so irresistible that they readily consent to a perpetual state of interruption as the new motivational status quo. Eliot could see nothing coming of this but lives "Filled with fancies and empty of meaning / Tumid apathy with no concentration."[21] However, a growing contingent of commentators regards hyper attention optimistically, as a learned form of cognitive dexterity necessary for survival, rather than as a dysfunctional state of distraction. For example, the author of a Kaiser Family Foundation report suggests that young people's ability to process multiple streams of information may be an inevitable evolutionary adaptation to the new reality:

> In this media-heavy world, it is likely that brains that are more adept at media multitasking will be passed along and these changes will be naturally selected. After all, information is power, and if one can process more information all at once, perhaps one can be more powerful.[22]

Proponents of this view argue that schooling must move to keep pace with the times. They insist that, given the disjunction between emergent ways of knowing unique to the Internet generation and teaching practices that fail to meet the needs of this cohort of learners, it is important for teachers to explore new, more appropriate pedagogies that exploit the fact that young people function best amidst multiple information streams. According to Prensky, for example, if "digital natives" are forsaking reflective habits of mind, it is because their altered learning preferences and styles are not being accommodated by their "digital immigrant" teachers.[23] In fact, as a slogan, "digital native" not only inaccurately paints all young people with the same brush but also creates a panicked sense that teachers and teaching must adapt. The refrain, repeated unreflectively in educational publications, at conferences, and in the emerging discourse of "twenty-first century learning," is that "we need to think in terms of transforming the educational experience so that it is meaningful to the information-age learner"[24]—or else be labelled as dinosaurs, unwilling and unable to keep up with the times.

Educational psychologist Jerome Bruner labels as "sentimentalism" this kind of knee-jerk assumption that teaching should always be fitted to the child's proclivities.[25] While I agree with Prensky that the demands and constraints of schooling, in general, are antithetical to reflection (more on this in the next chapter), I remain unconvinced that it is possible to reanimate reflective habits of mind by foregoing depth, deliberation, and abstract thought in favour of the technological wizardry and collaborative interaction that digital natives are said to prefer. As students create PowerPoint presentations (replete with hyperlinks and multimedia enhancements) and conduct research online (scanning digital texts or doing keyword searches rather than perusing books in depth), information access and technical virtuosity are inevitably elevated in the minds of both learners and teachers, while reflection is correspondingly diminished as a hallmark of intelligence and as a worthy end of education.

In this chapter, I have offered a counter perspective: the view that information technology is inherently inimical to reflection. Running to keep up with the endless flow of fascinating distractions, the sheer proliferation of media and messages, both teachers and students adopt a manic pace that makes it untenable and undesirable to simply stop and think. And as brains become increasingly habituated to rapid jumps from one task or information stream to another, the ability to sustain attention and to stop and think is further attenuated. This is all to the good if our goal is to produce efficient corporate automatons, but not if we are hoping our students will become thoughtful and discerning citizens.

The challenge, then, becomes finding ways to create learning experiences and environments that do not hyper-stimulate learners but minimize distractions and help them find focus. Rather than enlarging a communications culture in which uninterrupted moments for contemplation are increasingly hard to find, our task as teachers is to support the values of mindfulness and care.

I believe that the teacher's role with respect to technology is best described as one of stewardship. Rather than simply accepting, with either reluctance or enthusiasm, the arrival of the latest technological "tool," we must manage, with care and forethought, the movement of technological innovation into educational spaces. And rather than simply using these technologies to make our instruction more engaging, convenient, or relevant, it is imperative that the technologies themselves become the subject of instruction, opening up possibilities for discussion and reflection on how computers, cell phones, and other devices are altering the substance and tenor of human life. What does it mean, for example, when students sitting in the same room choose to email or text each other instead of conversing face-to-face? When instruction is reduced to bulleted points on a series of PowerPoint slides that students access online in lieu of attending class? When students open their laptops instead of a book when it comes time to read and complete assignments? Rather than celebrating a computer culture in which ubiquitous digital devices simply disappear from view, the teacher's role is to moderate change by attending reflectively to what is gained and lost in the process, and by including students in the discussion.

In the final chapter, I will pursue the question of education's role in sustaining the reflective intellect in a technological society that is overrun with eye-twitching distractions.

Chapter 7

CULTIVATING REFLECTIVENESS

> The cultivation of reflectiveness, or whatever you choose
> to call it, is one of the great problems one faces in deliver-
> ing curricula: how to lead children to discover the powers
> and pleasures that await the exercise of retrospection.[1]
>
> —Jerome Bruner

AS I APPROACH THE END OF MY REFLECTIONS ON REFLECTION,
I am compelled to return, for a moment, to the seminar room
in which I began, to the six teacher-students sitting around a
table, chuckling at the impossibility of reflection. Considering
that scenario again, I am struck by the fact that what was really
at issue, in that small moment, was a shared appreciation for the
disjunction between "schooling" and "education."

By schooling, I mean the reality in which teaching and
learning take place. As a product of the unique values and
beliefs of a specific group of people, schooling necessarily differs
across both time and space. In *Nineteen Eighty-Four*, George
Orwell plays with that variability, depicting a future society
(for him, writing in 1949) in which no one is aghast at the fact
that schooling entails what we would today call brainwashing.
But elsewhere, Orwell is also humorously critical of the real
schooling he endured in an English boarding school:

Over a period of two or three years the scholarship boys were crammed with learning as cynically as a goose is crammed for Christmas. And with what learning! . . . Your job was to learn exactly those things that would give an examiner the impression that you knew more than you did know, and as far as possible to avoid burdening your brain with anything else. . . . Latin and Greek, the main scholarship subjects, were what counted, but even these were deliberately taught in a flashy, unsound way. We never, for example, read right through even a single book of a Greek or Latin author: we merely read short passages which were picked out because they were the kind of thing likely to be set as an "unseen translation."[2]

This passage reinforces what I suggested in an earlier chapter: the processes and demands of schooling in our society are such that most teachers and learners have little time or motivation to stop and think. In *Thinking in Education,* Matthew Lipman goes further, asserting that contemporary schooling actually dulls children's naturally reflective minds, systematically draining them "of the capital fund of initiative and inventiveness and thoughtfulness that they brought with them to school."[3] So many aspects of schooling—from architectural designs that regulate, monitor, and normalize students, to assessments that require little more than factual recall—conspire to shut down any inclinations to reverie with which the child may arrive.

If "schooling" describes the pragmatic reality in which teachers and learners strive to impart and receive information— a reality that, in its emphasis on performance targets, tangible results, and accountability, tends to be antithetical to reflection—then "education," as I will use it here, embodies an ideal:

forms of teaching and learning, both formal and informal, that take place outside of institutional and ideological boundaries, and which serve to open and activate the reflective intellect. While the role of schooling is to inculcate the information and values that individuals will need in order to function as productive workers, the role of education is to promote in learners a predisposition to stop and think, and thereby to arrive at new insights, and new possibilities for themselves and their world. Educator and philosopher Maxine Greene eloquently articulates the distinction:

> We are interested in education here, not in schooling. We are interested in openings, in unexplored possibilities, not in the predictable or the quantifiable, not in what is thought of as social control. For us, education signifies an initiation into a new way of seeing, hearing, feeling, moving. It signifies the nurture of a special kind of reflectiveness and expressiveness, a reaching out for meaning, a learning to learn.[4]

Academia has long been considered a bastion for the reflective intellect, and for this reason it is customary to refer to what happens in universities not as schooling but as education; however, in post-secondary institutions established to cultivate the life of the mind, we find that increasing pressures from a neo-liberal agenda enforce a concern with outcomes, efficiencies, accountability, and preparing learners to compete successfully in the global marketplace. Our universities are therefore rapidly mutating, in the name of relevance and mere survival, into businesses, top-heavy with administrators, from which students may acquire credentials and job skills, but little else.

This means that many students graduate without having had to write an essay, without having entered the library, without having read anything other than the assigned pages of a textbook, and quite possibly without having had the need or perhaps even the opportunity to engage in reflective thought.

Nor is this true of the students alone: most institutions of higher learning are staffed by faculty members too dogged by their teaching and research responsibilities—by bulging email inboxes, incessant rounds of funding proposals, conference circuits, and the other unrelenting demands that accompany a "publish or perish" mentality—to pause for reflection themselves, or to encourage their students to do so. I am keenly aware of the irony that, while working on this book, I have found it enormously difficult to create an intellectual space in which it was possible to retreat, if only for a few hours here and there, in order to read, write, and think—to reflect on reflection.

The extreme fragmentation of scholarly thought further works against reflection by compelling both students and teachers to focus intently upon a single, highly specialized area of inquiry. Furthermore, thanks in large part to the demands of funding agencies, academic inquiry is increasingly undertaken with the goal of producing results that can be commercialized or otherwise applied to real-world situations. The desire to ponder questions about the world that defy definitive answers or obvious practical applications—the essence of scholarship—clearly does not fit within this mandate. Thus, even in academia, the realities of schooling intrude to the extent that reflection is quickly becoming devalued and inaccessible to both students and faculty as a means of understanding the world.

When the teachers sitting around that seminar table laughed, it was not at the idea of reflection, but its impossibility, given the impinging realities of schooling. Like most teachers, they function, professionally, somewhere in the grey area between the two binaries: struggling to educate while coping with the day-to-day realities and constraints of schooling. The indictment here is not of the practices of individual teachers but of the system within which we all teach and learn. It is a system that, at all levels, devalues reflection by privileging product over process and superficial coverage of curricular content over in-depth exploration. It does this by demanding that knowledge be fragmented and learning quantified, and by equating both academic success and instructional competence with the ability to provide the correct answer promptly rather than with taking the time to explore the kinds of questions that defy such certainties. No teacher goes into the classroom with the intention of dulling her students' reflective capabilities, but as we become caught up in the demands of schooling, it is easy to forget that our most important task, as educators, is what Jerome Bruner calls "the cultivation of reflectiveness."

One of the reasons, perhaps, for the popularity of Dewey's redefinition of reflection as scientific problem solving is that it fits so well with the dictates of schooling. Many common practices and products of schooling, from the organization of curricula and classrooms to the content of textbooks and examination questions, emerge from a similar view of knowledge as objective, structured, and verifiable. Furthermore, for educators hoping to take small steps away from *schooling* toward *education*, in which the primary goal is to nourish the reflective intellect, Dewey's notion of reflective thinking seems to provide a straightforward approach, a five-step plan that can be assiduously followed by even the busiest of teachers: state the problem, suggest possible solutions, evaluate the solutions, formulate a hypothesis, and test it.

Schön's notion of reflective practice has achieved a similar level of popularity among teachers, for similar reasons. By depicting the reflective practitioner as someone who mulls over his or her own preconceptions and teaching practices as part of a continuous process of professional self-improvement, Schön has placed reflection within reach of even the busiest educators. Schools and teacher education programs respond with attempts to create a "culture of reflection" by instituting lunch 'n' learn sessions, professional learning communities, study groups, professional development opportunities, and action research projects. While it is difficult to dispute the individual value of such measures, the cumulative effect is to set into motion a round of busyness that consumes the few remaining hours and opportunities already overworked teachers might have for reflection as I have defined it.

As should be clear by now, reflection as I define it is neither a tool nor process, neither an approach to problem solving nor a form of professional navel-gazing. It cannot be reduced to definitive steps and algorithms; indeed, as I suggested in an earlier chapter, it cannot be taught, because it is not simply a way of thinking but a way of *being*. I believe that it can, however, be fostered—or, as Bruner puts it, cultivated—by individual teachers.

* * *

I have now reached a point in my reflections when it is considered incumbent upon me to offer constructive suggestions and concrete recommendations for action and improvement in order to answer the "so what" questions that naturally arise in a society in which little merit is accorded to contemplative thought for its own sake. However, anyone hoping, at this point, for a set of specific guidelines will, I fear, be sorely disappointed. Of course, many books and articles *do* provide such guidelines and other straightforward advice on fostering reflection, but the semantically diminished forms of reflection to which they refer—reflection as a problem-solving process, a set of cognitive skills, a form of review, or self-examination—bear little resemblance to the sense of the word I have sought to reclaim. Moreover, such guidelines, though highly sought after by harried teachers, impede precisely the kind of thinking I have been advocating: deep, generative thought that takes place in conditions of silence and stillness.

In fact, the attentive reader will have already found, up to this point, many general suggestions for fostering reflective thought. For example, in previous chapters, I have touched upon the importance of being openly attentive to the way that words are used—particularly words that are integral to our understanding and experience of teaching and learning. Language, after all, is the basic material with which the reflective mind works. The unquestioning use of words that have become debased through mis- and overuse is like putting grit in the gears of the reflective intellect, causing it to slow, perhaps even grind to a halt. I have also emphasized the importance of developing an appreciation for the indeterminate products of the reflective intellect, which might be expressed by finding a way to accept the provisionality of questioning *by* learners as having a value at least commensurate with their ability to provide the right answers to questions asked *of* them. I have suggested the value of providing learners with ample opportunities for unassessed reading and writing, moments of silent withdrawal that are offered as privilege rather than punishment. I have referred to the importance of interdisciplinarity, which allows both teachers and learners to make connections that might be unavailable to those whose perspective is constrained by the boundaries of a single field of study. I have suggested that reflection not be consigned to the last few minutes of a lesson, as a tacked-on consolidation exercise, but that it occur, as reflection-then-action, within a lesson, allowing learners the opportunity to question, consolidate, and then take small, stumbling steps forward, engaging in activities and experiences that are informed by their reflections. I have emphasized the need to deliberately and actively make room for silence, as a counterweight to all the busyness and buzz, and the need to model an appreciation for moments of silence, rather than wielding it as a disciplinary tool or rushing to fill the acoustic void with noise and busywork. And, finally, I have suggested that technology become not the means of instruction but its subject—the focus of discussions and reflections about how new communications devices alter human interactions, habits of mind, and possibilities.

These are the kinds of small steps individuals can take in order to begin to enact change within continuity.

More in the way of specific recommendations is not possible because each situation is unique: it is impossible to prescribe reflection. Nor is it desirable, because prescriptions and step-by-step processes are calls to unreflective action, not to reflection.

In lieu of such guidelines, I offer the following brief story, which began some time ago when I gave a guest lecture to a group of university students. The students attending seemed to be interested in my topic and asked many intelligent questions; indeed, they were so interested that the class ran overtime. Two or three days later, I was rushing to a meeting when one of the students who had attended my presentation stopped me in the hallway. I remembered him: he had kept his head down throughout my talk and had not asked any questions. I had assumed from his posture in the class that he was uninterested in what I had to say, perhaps even dozing. Now, however, it seemed that he had a pressing question that he wanted to ask—a question he was having difficulty articulating as he stumblingly and circuitously spoke about a novel he had read, an article he had found, something that had come up in conversation with a family member, and how all of this somehow connected to a point I had raised in my presentation. As I listened, it became clear that he was making some new connections between all these pieces; I could almost see the synapses firing in his brain as he spoke. At that moment, I realized that I had a choice: I could stand and hear this student out, and try to help him articulate his reflections, or I could get to my meeting on time.

Let me just say that I held my ground and put aside the impulse to look at my watch.

The moral of my story is this: reflection *can* be cultivated— but only, I believe, by a teacher for whom reflection is an ethical commitment. For surely, it has to begin here: with opening our own minds to the intrinsic worth, for its own sake, of quiet moments of contemplation. How can I, as a teacher, hope to cultivate learners' appreciation for reflection if I do not give priority to deep, slow thought, and if I do not enter the classroom fully committed to the value of expressing, modelling, and, ultimately, reanimating a commitment to its intrinsic worth in my own and my students' daily lives?

CONCLUSION

I HAVE ATTEMPTED, IN THIS ESSAY, TO INITIATE A MUCH-NEEDED discussion about what reflection is and should be. The word crops up repeatedly in the discourse of teaching and learning, but its meaning is generally far from clear. Is it a form of action? A scientific process? An opportunity to review learning experiences? A reflexive contemplation of one's professional practice? I have suggested that it is none of these things. Rather, reflection, in the conventional sense that I have sought to reclaim, is a form of deep thought, emerging in conditions of solitude and slowness, in which the mind engages in a synthesizing process that tends to produce original ideas, insights, and perspectives. The rampant use and misuse of the term to refer to other forms of thought that are more congruent with the exigencies of modern society is a compelling sign that the reflection of solitude and slowness is in retreat—in life as in language.

When we unquestioningly accept such usages, we not only condone the authors' inroads into the conventional meaning of reflection; we also allow slow, silent reverie to fade from notice and, ultimately, to be wiped from the palette of pedagogical possibilities. Further, we risk blindly following those who misuse the word into pseudo-reflective practices—for example, requiring learners to complete so-called "structured reflection" activities or keep reflective learning journals—that may actually derail authentic reflection by reducing it, in the students' understanding and experience, to a step-by-step process or tedious labour over a make-work project for marks.

When, on the other hand, we insist upon mindfully and deliberately using reflection to refer to deep thought that takes place in conditions of solitude and slowness, we begin to reclaim it as a habit of mind that has a valuable role to play in teaching and learning, and in our lives. And with a new attentiveness to the nuances of usage—an attentiveness that is best shared with students—we may also begin to notice that other important words, such as "learning" and "intelligence," are often used in ways that privilege technological or rational ways of knowing over the kind of knowledge that is born of reflection.

I worry that this social devaluation of reflection presages its disappearance from our mental landscape. Just as reflection in solitude and silence is inextricably connected with the technologies of written language, so its decline can be linked to our contemporary communications culture, the sheer proliferation of media and messages. Running to keep up with the endless flow of fascinating distractions, we adopt a manic pace that makes it untenable and undesirable for us to simply stop and think. In the classroom, reflection is devolving into little more than a learning outcome that can be quantified, an item that the harried teacher ticks off on a checklist before proceeding at breakneck speed to the next. Increasingly, moments seized from the busyness of our daily round in which to simply stop and think are viewed as wasted time, idle moments of woolgathering.

It seems to me that we are now at a crucial juncture. Much depends on our ability as individuals and as a society to preserve at least the remnants of a non-instrumental definition of reflection, and, inherent within that meaning, an appreciation for reflection as a valued end in itself rather than as a means to more practical, tangible accomplishments. Educators have a particularly important role to play here: it is up to us not only to provide the space the reflective impulse needs in order to thrive, but also to model for our students a commitment to the value of contemplative thought. Reflection so valued nourishes the spirit, and may give rise to small actions that cumulatively enhance social balance and care.

My ultimate purpose, in this essay, has been to suggest that reflection, for its own sake, is a habit of mind—indeed, a way of being—that is worth preserving if we are to move with integrity and hope toward a livable future.

NOTES

Chapter 1: Reclaiming Reflection

1   Martin Heidegger, *What is called thinking?*, trans. Fred D. Wieck and J. Glenn Gray (New York: Harper & Row, 1968), 27.

2   Henry David Thoreau, *Walden: A fully annotated edition*, ed. Jeffrey S. Cramer (1854; reprint, New Haven: Yale University Press, 2004), 88.

3   Thoreau, *Walden*, 80.

4   Robert Pogue Harrison, *Gardens: An essay on the human condition* (Chicago: University of Chicago Press, 2008), 17–18.

5   Hannah Arendt, *Thinking,* vol. 1 of *The life of the mind* (London: Secker & Warburg, 1978), 6.

6   Hank Bromley, "Introduction: Data-driven democracy? Social assessment of educational computing," in *Education/Technology/Power: Educational computing as a social practice*, eds. Hank Bromley and Michael W. Apple (New York: SUNY Press, 1998), 17.

7   Marc Prensky, "H. Sapiens digital: From digital immigrants and digital natives to digital wisdom," *Innovate: Journal of Online Education* 5, no. 3 (2009). Retrieved from http://innovateonline.info.

8   Alberto Manguel, *A history of reading* (Toronto: Alfred A. Knopf, 1996), 296.

9   Heidegger, *Introduction to metaphysics*, trans. Gregory Fried and Richard Post (1959; reprint, New Haven: Yale University Press, 2000), 14.

10 Marc Prensky, "Digital natives, digital immigrants: Do they really think differently?" *On the Horizon* 9, no. 6 (2001b): 5.

11 Malcolm Murray and Nebojsa Kujundzic, *Critical reflection: A textbook for critical thinking* (Montreal: McGill-Queen's University Press, 2005), 4.

12 John Dewey, *How we think: A restatement of the relation of reflective thinking to the educative process* (Boston: D.C. Heath and Company, 1933), v.

13 Dewey, *How we think*, 7.

14 Dewey, *How we think*, 106.

15 Dewey, *How we think*, 100–101.

16 Dewey, *How we think*, 166.

17 Dewey, *How we think*, 107–111.

18 Arendt, *Thinking*, 6.

19 Dewey, *How we think*, 17.

20 Mortimer J. Adler, *How to read a book* (New York: Simon and Schuster, 1940), 44.

21 Dewey, *How we think*, 184.

22 Adler, *How to read a book*, 44.

23 Laurence Buermeyer, William Forbes Cooley, John J. Coss, Horace L. Friess, James Gutmann, Thomas Munro, Houston Peterson, John H. Randall, Jr., and Herbert W. Schneider, *An introduction to reflective thinking* (Boston: Houghton Mifflin Company, 1923), 2.

24 Henry Gordon Hullfish and Philip G. Smith, *Reflective thinking: The method of education* (New York: Dodd, Mead & Company, 1961), 36.

25 David Boud, Rosemary Keough, and David Walker, "What is reflection in learning?" in *Reflection: Turning experience into learning*, eds. Boud, Keough, and Walker (London: Kogan Page, 1985), 11.

26 Boud, Keough, and Walker, "What is reflection in learning?" 9.

27 Boud, Keough, and Walker, "What is reflection in learning?" 16.

28 Donald A. Schön, *The reflective practitioner: How professionals think in action* (New York: Basic Books, 1983), 21.

29 Paul Hendrickson, "A social critique of reflective reason: Relocating critical theory after Habermas and Foucault" (unpublished doctoral dissertation, University of Illinois at Urbana-Champaign, 2001), 3.

30 Arendt, *Thinking*, 78 (emphasis in original).

31 John J. Loughran, "Effective reflective practice: In search of meaning in learning about teaching," *Journal of Teacher Education* 53, no. 1 (2002): 33.

32 Uwe Pörksen, *Plastic words: The tyranny of a modular language*, trans. Jutta Mason and David Cayley (University Park, PA: Pennsylvania State University, 1995).

Chapter 2: Why Does Reflection Matter?

1   Douglas Adams, *The hitchhiker's guide to the galaxy* (New York: Harmony Books, 1979), 173.

2   Joseph Conrad, *The secret agent* (1907; reprint, London: Penguin Books, 1984), 40.

3   Maurice Merleau-Ponty, *Phenomenology of perception*, trans. Colin Smith (1958; reprint, London: Routledge, 2003), 207.

4   Martin Heidegger, *Discourse on thinking*, trans. John M. Anderson and E. Hans Freund (New York: Harper & Row, 1966), 53.

5   Lewis Mumford, *The pentagon of power* (New York: Harcourt Brace Jovanovich, 1964), 88.

6   Neil Postman, *Technopoly: The surrender of culture to technology* (New York: Vintage Books, 1992), 63.

7   Lewis Mumford, *Sketches from life: The early years* (New York: The Dial Press, 1982), 98.

8   Donald Miller, *Lewis Mumford: A life* (New York: Grove Press, 1989), 6.

9   Miller, *Lewis Mumford*, 6.

10 Lewis Mumford, *Technics and civilization* (New York: Harcourt, Brace and Company, 1934), 447.

11 Sven Birkerts, *The Gutenberg elegies: The fate of reading in an electronic age* (New York: Fawcett Columbine, 1995), 75.

12 Lewis Mumford, *Technics and human development* (New York: Harcourt Brace Jovanovich, Inc., 1966), 188.

13 Alfred North Whitehead, *The aims of education and other essays* (1929; reprint, New York: Mentor Books, 1964), 15.

14 Martin Heidegger, *The question concerning technology and other essays*, trans. William Lovitt (New York: Harper & Row, 1977), 181.

15 Stephen Kemmis, "Action research and the politics of reflection," in *Reflection: Turning experience into learning* (London: Kogan Page, 1985), 140.

16 Peter McLaren, *Life in schools: An introduction to critical pedagogy in the foundations of education* (New York: Longman, 1989), 233. (Emphasis in original.)

17 Mumford, *Technics and civilization*, 6.

18 Dick Pels, "Unhastening science: Temporal demarcations in the 'social triangle,'" *European Journal of Social Theory* 6, no. 2 (2003).

Chapter 3: The Rise of the Reflective Mind

1 Marshall McLuhan and Quentin Fiore, *The medium is the massage: An inventory of effects* (New York: Bantam Books, 1967), 48.

2 William Shakespeare, "King Lear," in *The Riverside Shakespeare*, edited by G. Blakemore Evans (Boston: Houghton Mifflin, 1974), IV.6.1287.

3 Denise Schmandt-Besserat, *From counting to cuneiform*, vol. 1 of *Before writing* (Austin: University of Texas Press, 1992), 177.

4 Schmandt-Besserat, *From counting to cuneiform*, 129.

5 David Abram, *The spell of the sensuous: Perception and language in a more-than-human world* (New York: Vintage, 1996), 255.

6 Edmund Carpenter, *Oh, what a blow that phantom gave me!* (New York: Holt, Rinehart and Winston, 1972), 37.

7 Edith Hamilton, *Mythology* (1942; reprint, New York: New American Library, 1969), 19.

8 Walter J. Ong, *Orality and literacy: The technologizing of the word* (London: Routledge, 1982), 42.

9 Francis Bacon, *Advancement of learning and Novum organum* (1605 and 1620; reprint, New York: The Colonial Press, 1900), 366.

10 David Riesman, "The oral and written traditions," in *Explorations in communication* (Boston: Beacon Press, 1960), 110.

11 Elizabeth L. Eisenstein, *The printing press as an agent of change*, vols. 1 and 2 (Cambridge: Cambridge University Press, 1979), 3.

12 Ivan Illich and Barry Sanders, *ABC: The alphabetization of the popular mind* (New York: Vintage, 1988), 46.

13 Ivan Illich, "A plea for research on lay literacy," *Interchange* 18, no. 1/2 (1987): 15.

14 Saint Augustine, *The confessions of Saint Augustine*, trans. Edward B. Pusey (397–400; reprint, New York: Random House, 1999), 98.

15 Riesman, "The oral and written traditions," 112.

16 Riesman, "The oral and written traditions," 114.

17 Ong, *Orality and literacy*, 49–55.

18 John Richetti, *The English novel in history: 1700–1780* (London: Routledge, 1999), 8.

19 Barry Sanders, *The private death of public discourse* (Boston: Beacon Press, 1998), 126.

20 Eisenstein, *The printing press as an agent of change*, 33.

Chapter 4: Reading, Writing, and Reflection

1 Ursula K. Le Guin, "Staying awake: Notes on the alleged decline of reading," *Harper's*, February 2008, 34.

2 Lionel Trilling, *The liberal imagination: Essays on literature and society* (New York: Harcourt Brace Jovanovich, 1950), 91.

3 David Paul Nord, "A republican literature: A study of magazine reading and readers in late eighteenth-century New York," *American Quarterly* 40, no. 1 (1988).

4 Thomas Hardy, *Jude the obscure* (1896; reprint, London: MacMillan, 1974), 86.

5 George Steiner, *In Bluebeard's castle: Some notes towards the re-definition of culture* (London: Faber & Faber, 1971), 86.

6 Jacques Ellul, *The humiliation of the word*, trans. Joyce Main Hanks (1981; reprint, Grand Rapids: William B. Eerdmans, 1985), 117.

7 Ellul, *The humiliation of the word*, 219.

8 Sven Birkerts, "Notes from a confession," in *Reading in bed: Personal essays on the glories of reading*, ed. Steven Gilbar (Boston: David R. Godine, 1996), 144.

9 Pat Belanoff, "Silence: Reflection, literacy, learning, and teaching," *College Composition and Communication* 52, no. 3 (2001): 413.

10 Maryanne Wolf, *Proust and the squid: The story and science of the reading brain* (New York: Harper Perennial, 2007), 17–18.

11 Marcel Proust, *On reading*, trans. Jean Autret and William Burford (1906; reprint, New York: Macmillan, 1971), 43.

12 Proust, *On reading*, 43.

13 Dewey, *How we think*, 257.

14 Heather Menzies and Janice Newson, "No time to think: Academics' life in the globally wired university," *Time & Society* 16, no. 1 (2007), 90.

15 James Moffett, "Writing, inner speech, and meditation," *College English* 44, no. 3 (1982): 231.

16 Moffett, "Writing, inner speech, and meditation," 234.

17 William Shakespeare, "Romeo and Juliet," in *The Riverside Shakespeare*, edited by G. Blakemore Evans (Boston: Houghton Mifflin, 1974) II.2.3–4, 1068.

18 Research confirms that mandated reflective journaling is not an effective strategy for promoting reflection. See, for example, Janet E. Dyment and Timothy S. O'Connell, "The quality of reflection in student journals: A review of limiting and enabling factors," *Journal of Innovative Higher Education* 35, no. 4 (2010); Valerie Hobbs, "Faking it or hating it: Can reflective practice be forced?" *Reflective Practice: International and Multidisciplinary Perspectives* 8, no. 3 (2007).

Chapter 5: Is Reflection in Decline?

1 Alberto Manguel, *The city of words* (Toronto: Anansi, 2007), 69.

2 Manguel, *The city of words*, 127.

3 David Geoffrey Smith, *Pedagon: Interdisciplinary essays in human sciences, pedagogy and culture* (New York: Peter Lang, 1999), 5.

4 Heidegger, *Discourse on thinking*, 44–45.

5 Heidegger, *Discourse on thinking*, 45.

6 Heidegger, *Discourse on thinking*, 46.

7 Ong, *Orality and literacy*, 137.

8 George Orwell, "Politics and the English Language," *A collection of essays* (San Diego: Harcourt, 1946), 159.

9 John Ralston Saul, *Voltaire's bastards: The dictatorship of reason in the West* (Toronto: Penguin, 1992), 49.

10 Edward R. Tufte, *The cognitive style of PowerPoint* (Cheshire: Graphics Press, 2003), 26.

11 Ronna Scott Mosher, "Silence, listening, teaching, and the space of what is not," *Language Arts* 78, no. 4 (2001), 368.

12 Smith, *Pedagon*, 55–56.

13 Smith, *Pedagon*, 24.

14 Plato, *Plato's Phaedrus* (Cambridge: Cambridge University Press, 1952), 157.

15 Jane Healy, *Failure to connect: How computers affect our children's minds—for better and worse* (New York: Simon & Schuster, 1998), 167.

16 William Barrett, *The illusion of technique* (1967; reprint, New York: Anchor Press, 1978), 222–223.

Chapter 6: Reflection and Technology

1 Gary Small and Gigi Vorgan, *iBrain: Surviving the technological alteration of the modern mind* (New York: HarperCollins, 2008); Lianne George, "Dumbed down: The troubling science of how technology is rewiring kids' brains," *Maclean's*, November 2008, 56–59; Mark Bauerlein, *The dumbest generation: How the digital age stupefies young Americans and jeopardizes our future (or, don't trust anyone under 30)* (New York: Penguin, 2008); Nicholas Carr, *The shallows: What the Internet is doing to our brains* (New York: W.W. Norton & Company, 2010); Nicholas Carr, "Is Google making us stupid?" *Atlantic* 302, July/August 2008, 56–63.

2 Carr, "Is Google making us stupid?" 57.

3 For an excellent analysis of the discrepancy between Bush's vision and the accelerating effects of information technology see David M. Levy, "No time to think: Reflections on information technology and contemplative scholarship," *Ethics and Information Technology* 9, no. 4 (2007): 237–249.

4 Vannevar Bush, "As we may think," *Atlantic*, July 1945, 106–107.

5 Bush, "As we may think," 101.

6 Bush, "As we may think," 104.

7 Paul Levinson, *The soft edge: A natural history and future of the information revolution* (London: Routledge, 1997), 164.

8   Sue Ferguson, "How computers make our kids stupid," *Maclean's*, 6 June 2005, 24.

9   Michael Horsnell, "Why texting harms your IQ," *The Times*, 22 April 2005.

10 Postman, *Technopoly*, 68.

11 Tom Standage, *The Victorian Internet: The remarkable story of the telegraph and the nineteenth century's on-line pioneers* (New York: Walker and Company, 1998), 49.

12 Postman, *Technopoly*, 69–70.

13 N. Katherine Hayles, "Hyper and deep attention: The generational divide in cognitive modes," *Profession* 13, (2007).

14 Linda Stone, "Continuous partial attention," accessed Jan. 1, 2008, http://www.lindastone.net/qa/continuous-partial-attention/.

15 Hayles, "Hyper and deep attention," 187.

16 Ulla G. Foehr, *Media multitasking among American youth: Prevalence, predictors and pairings* (Menlo Park, CA: Henry J. Kaiser Family Foundation, 2006), 15.

17 Ong, *Orality and literacy*, 132.

18 This is a meme offered by Prensky in Rachel Dretzin, producer, "Digital nation: Life on the virtual frontier" [Television series episode]. *Frontline*. Boston: WGBH, 2010.

19 Ellen Rose, *University students' experiences of media multitasking during online learning*, paper presented at the annual meeting of the Canadian Network for Innovation in Education (Saint John, NB: CNIE, 2010).

20 Ellen Rose, "The phenomenology of on-screen reading: University students' experience of digitised text," *British Journal of Educational Technology* 42, no. 3 (2011).

21 T.S. Eliot, *Collected poems 1909–1962* (London: Faber & Faber, 1963), 192–193.

22 Foehr, *Media multitasking among American youth*, 24.

23 Marc Prensky, "Digital natives, digital immigrants," *On the Horizon* 9, no. 5 (2001a).

24 Jason L. Frand, "The information-age mindset: Changes in students and implications for higher education," *EDUCAUSE Review* 35, no. 5 (2000), 24.

25 Jerome Bruner, *On knowing: Essays for the left hand* (Cambridge: Belknap Press of Harvard University Press, 1962), 117.

Chapter 7: Cultivating Reflectiveness

1   Jerome Bruner, *Beyond the information given: Studies in the psychology of knowing* (New York: W.W. Norton & Company, 1973), 449.

2   George Orwell, "Such, such were the joys …," in *A collection of essays* (San Diego: Harcourt, 1981), 8.

3   Matthew Lipman, *Thinking in education*, 2nd ed. (West Nyack, NY: Cambridge University Press, 2003), 13.

4   Maxine Greene, *Variations on a blue guitar: The Lincoln Center Institute lectures on aesthetic education* (New York: Teachers College Press, 2001), 7.

BIBLIOGRAPHY

Abram, David. *The spell of the sensuous: Perception and language in a more-than-human world*. New York: Vintage, 1996.

Adams, Douglas. *The hitchhiker's guide to the galaxy*. New York: Harmony Books, 1979.

Adler, Mortimer J. *How to read a book*. New York: Simon and Schuster, 1940.

Arendt, Hannah. *Thinking*. Vol. 1 of *The life of the mind*. London: Secker & Warburg, 1978.

Augustine, Saint. *The confessions of Saint Augustine*. Translated by Edward B. Pusey. 397–400. Reprinted, New York: Random House, 1999.

Bacon, Francis. *Advancement of learning and Novum organum*. 1605 and 1620. Reprint, New York: The Colonial Press, 1900.

Barrett, William. *The illusion of technique*. 1967. Reprinted, New York: Anchor Press, 1978.

Bauerlein, Mark. *The dumbest generation: How the digital age stupefies young Americans and jeopardizes our future (or, don't trust anyone under 30)*. New York: Penguin, 2008.

Belanoff, Pat. "Silence: Reflection, literacy, learning, and teaching." *College Composition and Communication* 52, no. 3 (2001): 399–428.

Birkerts, Sven. *The Gutenberg elegies: The fate of reading in an electronic age*. New York: Fawcett Columbine, 1995.

Birkerts, Sven. "Notes from a confession." In *Reading in bed: Personal essays on the glories of reading*, edited by Steven Gilbar. Boston: David R. Godine, 1996.

Boud, David, Rosemary Keough, and David Walker. "What is reflection in learning?" In *Reflection: Turning experience into learning*, edited by Boud, Keough, and Walker, 7–17. London: Kogan Page, 1985.

Bromley, Hank. "Introduction: Data-driven democracy? Social assessment of educational computing." In *Education/Technology/Power: Educational computing as a social practice*, edited by Hank Bromley and Michael W. Apple, 1–25. New York: SUNY Press, 1998.

Bruner, Jerome. *On knowing: Essays for the left hand*. Cambridge: The Belknap Press of Harvard University Press, 1962.

Bruner, Jerome. *Beyond the information given: Studies in the psychology of knowing*. New York: W.W. Norton & Company, 1973.

Buermeyer, Laurence, William Forbes Cooley, John J. Coss, Horace L. Friess, James Gutmann, Thomas Munro, Houston Peterson, John H. Randall, Jr., and Herbert W. Schneider. *An introduction to reflective thinking.* Boston: Houghton Mifflin Company, 1923.

Bush, Vannevar. "As we may think." *Atlantic,* July 1945, 101–108.

Carpenter, Edmund. *Oh, what a blow that phantom gave me!* New York: Holt, Rinehart and Winston, 1972.

Carr, Nicholas. "Is Google making us stupid?" *Atlantic,* July/August 2008, 56–63.

Carr, Nicholas. *The shallows: What the Internet is doing to our brains.* New York: W.W. Norton & Company, 2010.

Conrad, Joseph. *The secret agent.* 1907. Reprinted, London: Penguin Books, 1984.

Department of Canadian Heritage. *The book retail sector in Canada.* September 2007.

Dewey, John. *How we think: A restatement of the relation of reflective thinking to the educative process.* 1910. Reprinted, Boston: D.C. Heath and Company, 1933.

"Digital nation: Life on the virtual frontier." Produced by Rachel Dretzin. Boston: WGBH, 2010. Television documentary for *Frontline.*

Dyment, Janet E., and Timothy S. O'Connell. "The quality of reflection in student journals: A review of limiting and enabling factors." *Innovative Higher Education* 35, no. 4 (2010): 233–244.

Eisenstein, Elizabeth L. *The printing press as an agent of change.* Vols. 1 and 2. Cambridge: Cambridge University Press, 1979.

Eliot, T.S. *Collected Poems 1909–1962.* London: Faber & Faber, 1963.

Ellul, Jacques. *The technological society.* Translated by John Wilkinson. 1954. Reprinted, New York: Vintage Books, 1964.

Ellul, Jacques. *The technological system.* Translated by Joachim Neugroschel. 1977. Reprinted, New York: Continuum Publishing Company, 1980.

Ellul, Jacques. *The humiliation of the word.* Translated by Joyce Main Hanks. 1981. Reprinted, Grand Rapids: William B. Eerdmans, 1985.

Ferguson, Sue. "How computers make our kids stupid." *Maclean's,* 6 June 2005, 24–30.

Foehr, Ulla G. *Media multitasking among American youth: Prevalence, predictors and pairings.* Menlo Park, Calif.: Henry J. Kaiser Family Foundation, 2006.

Frand, Jason L. The information-age mindset: Changes in students and implications for higher education. *EDUCAUSE Review* 35, no. 5 (2000): 15–24.

George, Lianne. "Dumbed down: The troubling science of how technology is rewiring kids' brains." *Maclean's,* 17 November 2008, 56–59.

Gladwell, Malcolm. *Blink: The power of thinking without thinking*. New York: Little, Brown and Company, 2005.

Greene, Maxine. *Variations on a blue guitar: The Lincoln Center Institute lectures on aesthetic education*. New York: Teachers College Press, 2001.

Hamilton, Edith. *Mythology*. 1942. Reprinted, New York: New American Library, 1969.

Hardy, Thomas. *Jude the obscure*. 1896. Reprinted, London: MacMillan, 1974.

Harrison, Robert Pogue. *Gardens: An essay on the human condition*. Chicago: University of Chicago Press, 2008.

Hayles, N. Katherine. "Hyper and deep attention: The generational divide in cognitive modes." *Profession* 13, (2007): 187–199.

Healy, Jane. *Failure to connect: How computers affect our children's minds—for better and worse*. New York: Simon & Schuster, 1998.

Heidegger, Martin. *Discourse on thinking*. Translated by John M. Anderson and E. Hans Freund. New York: Harper & Row, 1966.

Heidegger, Martin. *What is called thinking?* Translated by Fred D. Wieck and J. Glenn Gray. New York: Harper & Row, 1968.

Heidegger, Martin. *The question concerning technology and other essays*. Translated by William Lovitt. New York: Harper & Row, 1977.

Heidegger, Martin. *Introduction to metaphysics*. Translated by Gregory Fried and Richard Post. 1959. Reprinted, New Haven: Yale University Press, 2000.

Hendrickson, Paul. "A social critique of reflective reason: Relocating critical theory after Habermas and Foucault." Doctoral dissertation, University of Illinois at Urbana-Champaign, 2001.

Hobbs, Valerie. "Faking it or hating it: Can reflective practice be forced?" *Reflective Practice: International and Multidisciplinary Perspectives* 8, no. 3 (2007): 405–417.

Horsnell, Michael. "Why texting harms your IQ." *The Times*, 22 April 2005.

Hullfish, Henry Gordon, and Philip G. Smith. *Reflective thinking: The method of education*. New York: Dodd, Mead, and Company, 1961.

Illich, Ivan. "A plea for research on lay literacy." *Interchange* 18, no. 1/2 (1987): 9–22.

Illich, Ivan, and Barry Sanders. *ABC: The alphabetization of the popular mind*. New York: Vintage, 1988.

Kemmis, Stephen. "Action research and the politics of reflection." In *Reflection: Turning experience into learning*, edited by David Boud, Rosemary Keough, and David Walker, 139–165. London: Kogan Page, 1985.

"Kids and family reading report: Turning the page in the digital age." Scholastic, 2010. Retrieved from http://mediaroom.scholastic.com/themes/bare_bones/2010_KFRR.pdf.

Le Guin, Ursula K. "Staying awake: Notes on the alleged decline of reading." *Harper's*, February 2008, 33–38.

Levinson, Paul. *The soft edge: A natural history and future of the information revolution*. London: Routledge, 1997.

Levy, David M. "No time to think: Reflections on information technology and contemplative scholarship." *Ethics and Information Technology* 9, no. 4 (2007): 237–249.

Lipman, Matthew. *Thinking in education*. 2nd ed. West Nyack, N.Y.: Cambridge University Press, 2003.

Locke, John. *An essay concerning human understanding*, edited by Peter H. Nidditch. 1690. Reprinted, Oxford: Clarendon Press, 1975.

Loughran, John J. "Effective reflective practice: In search of meaning in learning about teaching." *Journal of Teacher Education* 53, no. 1 (2002): 33–43.

Manguel, Alberto. *A history of reading*. Toronto: Alfred A. Knopf, 1996.

Manguel, Alberto. *The city of words*. Toronto: Anansi, 2007.

McLaren, Peter. *Life in schools: An introduction to critical pedagogy in the foundations of education*. New York: Longman, 1989.

McLuhan, Marshall, and Quentin Fiore. *The medium is the massage: An inventory of effects*. New York: Bantam Books, 1967.

Menzies, Heather. *No time: Stress and the crisis of modern life*. Vancouver: Douglas & McIntyre, 2005.

Menzies, Heather, and Janice Newson. "No time to think: Academics' life in the globally wired university." *Time & Society* 16, no. 1 (2007): 83–98.

Merleau-Ponty, Maurice. *Phenomenology of perception*. Translated by Colin Smith. 1958. Reprinted, London: Routledge, 2003.

Miller, Donald. *Lewis Mumford: A life*. New York: Grove Press, 1989.

Moffett, James. "Writing, inner speech, and meditation." *College English* 44, no. 3 (1982): 231–46.

Mosher, Ronna Scott. "Silence, listening, teaching, and the space of what is not." *Language Arts* 78, no. 4 (2001): 366–370.

Mumford, Lewis. *Technics and civilization*. New York: Harcourt, Brace and Company, 1934.

Mumford, Lewis. *The pentagon of power*. New York: Harcourt Brace Jovanovich, 1964.

Mumford, Lewis. *Technics and human development*. New York: Harcourt Brace Jovanovich, 1966.

Mumford, Lewis. *Sketches from life: The early years*. New York: The Dial Press, 1982.

Murray, Malcolm, and Nebojsa Kujundzic. *Critical reflection: A textbook for critical thinking*. Montreal: McGill-Queen's University Press, 2005.

National Endowment for the Arts. *To read or not to read: A question of national consequence*. Washington, D.C.: National Endowment for the Arts, 2007.

Nord, David Paul. "A republican literature: A study of magazine reading and readers in late eighteenth-century New York." *American Quarterly* 40, no. 1 (1988): 42–64.

Ong, Walter J. *Orality and literacy: The technologizing of the word.* London: Routledge, 1982.

Orwell, George. *A collection of essays.* San Diego: Harcourt, 1981.

Pels, Dick. "Unhastening science: Temporal demarcations in the 'social triangle.'" *European Journal of Social Theory* 6, no. 2 (2003): 209–231.

Piaget, Jean. "The stages of intellectual development in childhood and adolescence." In *The essential Piaget,* edited by Howard E. Gruber and J. Jacques Vonèche, 814–819. New York: Basic Books, 1977.

Plato. *Plato's Phaedrus.* Translated by R. Hackforth. Cambridge: Cambridge University Press, 1952.

Pörksen, Uwe. *Plastic words: The tyranny of a modular language.* Translated by Jutta Mason and David Cayley. University Park, Pa.: Pennsylvania State University, 1995.

Postman, Neil. *Technopoly: The surrender of culture to technology.* New York: Vintage Books, 1992.

Prensky, Marc. "Digital natives, digital immigrants." *On the Horizon* 9, no. 5 (2001a).

Prensky, Marc. "Digital natives, digital immigrants: Do they really think differently?" *On the Horizon* 9, no. 6 (2001b).

Prensky, Marc. "H. Sapiens digital: From digital immigrants and digital natives to digital wisdom." *Innovate: Journal of Online Education* 5, no. 3 (2009). http://innovateonline.info/

Proust, Marcel. *On reading.* Translated by Jean Autret and William Burford. 1906. Reprinted, New York: MacMillan, 1971.

Richetti, John. *The English novel in history: 1700–1780.* London: Routledge, 1999.

Riesman, David. "The oral and written traditions." In *Explorations in communication,* edited by Marshall McLuhan and Edmund Carpenter, 109–116. Boston: Beacon Press, 1960.

Rose, Ellen. "University students' experiences of media multitasking during online learning." Paper presented at the annual meeting of the Canadian Network for Innovation in Education in Saint John, NB, 2010.

Rose, Ellen. "The phenomenology of on-screen reading: University students' experience of digitised text." *British Journal of Educational Technology* 42, no. 3 (2011): 515–526.

Sanders, Barry. *The private death of public discourse.* Boston: Beacon Press, 1998.

Saul, John Ralston. *Voltaire's bastards: The dictatorship of reason in the West.* Toronto: Penguin, 1992.

Schmandt-Besserat, Denise. *From counting to cuneiform.* Vol. 1 of *Before writing.* Austin: University of Texas Press, 1992.

Schön, Donald A. *The reflective practitioner: How professionals think in action.* New York: Basic Books, 1983.

Shakespeare, William. "King Lear." In *The Riverside Shakespeare,* edited by G. Blakemore Evans, 1255–1295. Boston: Houghton Mifflin, 1974.

Shakespeare, William. "Romeo and Juliet." In *The Riverside Shakespeare,* edited by G. Blakemore Evans, 1058–1093. Boston: Houghton Mifflin, 1974.

Small, Gary, and Gigi Vorgan. *iBrain: Surviving the technological alteration of the modern mind.* New York: Harper Collins, 2008.

Smith, David Geoffrey. *Pedagon: Interdisciplinary essays in the human sciences, pedagogy and culture.* New York: Peter Lang, 1999.

Standage, Tom. *The Victorian Internet: The remarkable story of the telegraph and the nineteenth century's on-line pioneers.* New York: Walker and Company, 1998.

Steiner, George. *In Bluebeard's castle: Some notes towards the re-definition of culture.* London: Faber & Faber, 1971.

Stone, Linda. (2005). "Continuous partial attention." Retrieved Jan. 1, 2008 from http://www.lindastone.net/qa/continuous-partial-attention.

Thoreau, Henry David. *Walden: A fully annotated edition,* edited by Jeffrey S. Cramer. 1854. Reprinted, New Haven: Yale University Press, 2004.

Trilling, Lionel. "The function of the little magazine." In *The liberal imagination: Essays on literature and society,* 89–99. New York: Harcourt Brace Jovanovich, 1950.

Tufte, Edward R. *The cognitive style of PowerPoint.* Cheshire, Conn.: Graphics Press, 2003.

Whitehead, Alfred North. *The aims of education and other essays.* 1929. Reprinted, New York: Mentor Books, 1964.

Wolf, Maryanne. *Proust and the squid: The story and science of the reading brain.* New York: Harper Perennial, 2007.

INDEX